I0020346

# Serverless Architectures with AWS

Discover how you can migrate from traditional deployments to serverless architectures with AWS

Mohit Gupta

## Serverless Architectures with AWS

Copyright © 2018 Packt Publishing

All rights reserved. No part of this book may be reproduced, stored in a retrieval system, or transmitted in any form or by any means, without the prior written permission of the publisher, except in the case of brief quotations embedded in critical articles or reviews.

Every effort has been made in the preparation of this book to ensure the accuracy of the information presented. However, the information contained in this book is sold without warranty, either express or implied. Neither the author, nor Packt Publishing, and its dealers and distributors will be held liable for any damages caused or alleged to be caused directly or indirectly by this book.

Packt Publishing has endeavored to provide trademark information about all of the companies and products mentioned in this book by the appropriate use of capitals. However, Packt Publishing cannot guarantee the accuracy of this information.

Author: Mohit Gupta

Reviewer: Amandeep Singh

Managing Editor: Edwin Moses

Acquisitions Editor: Aditya Date

Production Editor: Nitesh Thakur

Editorial Board: David Barnes, Ewan Buckingham, Simon Cox, Manasa Kumar, Alex Mazonowicz, Douglas Paterson, Dominic Pereira, Shiny Poojary, Saman Siddiqui, Erol Staveley, Ankita Thakur, and Mohita Vyas.

First Published: December 2018

Production Reference: 1211218

Published by Packt Publishing Ltd.

Livery Place, 35 Livery Street

Birmingham B3 2PB, UK

ISBN 978-1-78980-502-4

*To my children, Aarya and Naisha.*

# Table of Contents

# Serverless Amazon Athena and the AWS Glue Data Catalog 99

# Real-Time Data Insights Using Amazon Kinesis 123

# Preface

## About

This section briefly introduces the author and reviewer, the coverage of this book, the technical skills you'll need to get started, and the hardware and software required to complete all of the included activities and exercises.

## About the Book

*Serverless Architectures with AWS* begins with an introduction to the serverless model and helps you get started with AWS and AWS Lambda. You'll also get to grips with other capabilities of the AWS serverless platform and see how AWS supports enterprise-grade serverless applications with and without Lambda.

This book will guide you through deploying your first serverless project and exploring the capabilities of Amazon Athena, an interactive query service that makes it easy to analyze data in Amazon Simple Storage Service (Amazon S3) using standard SQL. You'll also learn about AWS Glue, a fully managed extract, transfer, and load (ETL) service that makes categorizing data easy and cost-effective. You'll study how Amazon Kinesis makes it possible to unleash the potential of real-time data insights and analytics with capabilities such as Kinesis Data Streams, Kinesis Data Firehose, and Kinesis Data Analytics. Last but not least, you'll be equipped to combine Amazon Kinesis capabilities with AWS Lambda to create lightweight serverless architectures.

By the end of the book, you will be ready to create and run your first serverless application that takes advantage of the high availability, security, performance, and scalability of AWS.

## About the Author and Reviewer

**Mohit Gupta** is a solutions architect, focused on cloud technologies and Big Data analytics. He has more than 12 years of experience in IT and has worked on AWS and Azure technologies since 2012. He has helped customers design, build, migrate, and manage their workloads and applications on various cloud-based products, including AWS and Azure. He received his B.Tech in Computer Science from Kurukshetra University in 2005. Additionally, he holds many industry-leading IT certifications. You can reach him on LinkedIn at mogupta84 or follow his twitter handle **@mogupta**.

**Amandeep Singh** works as a distinguished Engineer with Pitney Bowes India Pvt Ltd. He has extensive development experience of more than 13 years in product companies like Pitney Bowes and Dell R&D center. His current role involves designing cloud based distributed solutions at enterprise scale. He is a AWS certified Solutions Architect, and helps Pitney Bowes migrate large monolith platform to AWS Cloud in the form of simpler and smarter microservices. He is strong believer of new age DevOps principles and microservices patterns. He can be reached on LinkedIn at bhatiaamandeep.

## Objectives

- Explore AWS services for supporting a serverless environment
- Set up AWS services to make applications scalable and highly available
- Deploy a static website with a serverless architecture
- Build your first serverless web application
- Study the changes in a deployed serverless web application
- Apply best practices to ensure overall security, availability, and reliability

## Audience

*Serverless Architectures with* AWS is for you if you want to develop serverless applications and have some prior coding experience. Though no prior experience of AWS is needed, basic knowledge of Java or Node.js will be an advantage.

## Approach

*Serverless Architectures with* AWS takes a hands-on approach to learning how to design and deploy serverless architectures. It contains multiple activities that use real-life business scenarios for you to practice and apply your new skills in a highly relevant context.

## Hardware Requirements

For an optimal student experience, we recommend the following hardware configuration:

- Processor: Intel Core i5 or equivalent
- Memory: 4 GB RAM
- Storage: 35 GB available space

## Software Requirements

You'll also need the following software installed in advance:

- Operating system: Windows 7 or above
- AWS Free Tier account
- Network access on ports 22 and 80

## Conventions

Code words in text, database table names, folder names, filenames, file extensions, pathnames, dummy URLs, user input, and Twitter handles are shown as follows: "You can also copy this code from the **s3_with_lambda.js** file."

A block of code is set as follows:

```
var AWS = require('aws-sdk');
var s3 = new AWS.S3();
```

New terms and important words are shown in bold. Words that you see on the screen, for example, in menus or dialog boxes, appear in the text like this: "Click on **Next** and follow the instructions to create the bucket."

## Additional Resources

The code bundle for this book is also hosted on GitHub at https://github.com/TrainingByPackt/Serverless-Architectures-with-AWS.

We also have other code bundles from our rich catalog of books and videos available at https://github.com/PacktPublishing/. Check them out!

# 1

# AWS, Lambda, and Serverless Applications

**Learning Objectives**

By the end of this chapter, you will be able to:

- Explain the serverless model
- Describe the different AWS serverless services present in the AWS ecosystem
- Create and execute an AWS Lambda function

This chapter teaches you the basics of serverless architectures, focusing on AWS.

## Introduction

Imagine that a critical application in your company is having performance issues. This application is available to customers 24-7, and during business hours, the CPU and memory utilization reaches 100%. This is resulting in an increased response time for customers.

Around 10 years ago, a good migration plan to solve this issue would involve the procurement and deployment of new hardware resources for both the application and its databases, the installation of all required software and application code, performing all functional and performance quality analysis work, and finally, migrating the application. The cost of this would run into millions. However, nowadays, this issue can be resolved with new technologies that offer different approaches to customers – *going Serverless* is definitely one of them.

In this chapter, we'll start with an explanation of the serverless model, and get started with AWS and Lambda, the building blocks of a serverless applications on AWS. Finally, you'll learn how to create and run Lambda functions.

## The Serverless Model

To understand the serverless model, let's first understand how we build traditional applications such as mobile applications and web applications. Figure 1.1 shows a traditional on-premises architecture, where you would take care of every layer of application development and the deployment process, starting with setting up hardware, software installation, setting up a database, networking, middleware configuration, and storage setup. Moreover, you would need a staff of engineers to set up and maintain this kind of on-premises setup, making it very time-consuming and costly. Moreover, the life cycle of these servers was no longer than 5-6 years, which meant that you would end up upgrading your infrastructure every few years.

The work wouldn't end there, as you would have to perform regular server maintenance, including setting up server reboot cycles and running regular patch updates. And despite doing all the groundwork and making sure that the system ran fine, the system would actually fail and cause application downtime. The following diagram shows a traditional on-premises architecture:

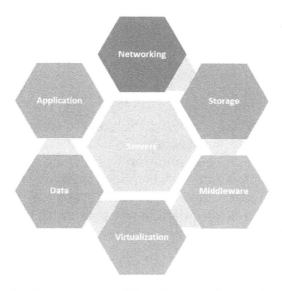

Figure 1.1 : Diagram of traditional on-premises architecture

The serverless model changes this paradigm completely, as it abstracts all the complexity attached with provisioning and managing data centers, servers, and software. Let's understand it in more detail.

The serverless model refers to applications in which server management and operational tasks are completely hidden from end users, such as developers. In the serverless model, developers are dedicated specifically to business code and the application itself, and they do not need to care about the servers where the application will be executed or run from, or about the performance of those servers, or any restrictions on them. The serverless model is scalable and is actually very flexible. With the serverless model, you focus on things that are more important to you, which is most probably solving business problems. The serverless model allows you to focus on your application architecture without you needing to think about servers.

Sometimes, the term "serverless" can be confusing. Serverless does not mean that you don't need any servers at all, but that you are not doing the work of provisioning servers, managing software, and installing patches. The term "the serverless model" just means that it is someone else's servers. Serverless architectures, if implemented properly, can provide great advantages in terms of lowering costs and providing operational excellence, thus improving overall productivity. However, you have to be careful when dealing with the challenges imposed by serverless frameworks. You need to make sure that your application doesn't have issues with performance, resource bottlenecks, or security.

*Figure* 1.2 shows the different services that are part of the serverless model. Here, we have different services for doing different kinds of work. We have the API Gateway service, a fully managed REST interface, which helps to create, publish, maintain, monitor, and secure APIs. Then, we have the AWS Lambda service that executes the application code and does all the computation work. Once computation is done, data gets stored in the DynamoDB database, which is again a fully managed service that provides a fast and scalable database management system. We also have the S3 storage service, where you can store all your data in raw formats that can be used later for data analytics. The following diagram talks about the serverless model:

## Serverless Model

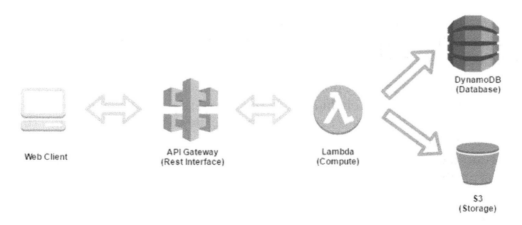

Figure 1.2 : The serverless model (using AWS services)

Serverless models have become quite popular in recent times, and many big organizations have moved their complete infrastructure to serverless architectures and have been running them successfully, getting better performance a much a lower cost. Many serverless frameworks have been designed, making it easier to build, test, and deploy serverless applications. However, our focus in this book will be on serverless solutions built on **Amazon Web Services** (**AWS**). Amazon Web Services is a subsidiary of Amazon.com that provides on-demand cloud service platforms.

## Benefits of the Serverless Model

There are a number of benefits to using a serverless model:

- **No server management**: Provisioning and managing servers is a complex task and it can take anything from days to months to provision and test new servers before you can start using them. If not done properly, and with a specific timeline, it can become a potential obstacle for the release of your software onto the market. Serverless models provide great relief here by masking all the system engineering work from the project development team.

- **High availability and fault tolerance**: Serverless applications have built-in architecture that supports **high availability** (**HA**). So, you don't need to worry about the implementation of these capabilities. For example, AWS uses the concept of regions and availability zones to maintain the high availability of all AWS services. An availability zone is an isolated location inside a region and you can develop your application in such a way that, if one of the availability zones goes down, your application will continue to run from another availability zone.

- **Scalability**: We all want our applications to be successful, but we need to make sure that we are ready when there is an absolute need for scaling. Obviously, we don't want to spawn very big servers in the beginning (since this can escalate costs quickly), but we want to do it as and when the need occurs. With serverless models, you can scale your applications very easily. Serverless models run under the limits defined by you, so you can easily expand those limits in the future. You can adjust the computing power, the memory, or IO needs of your application with just a few clicks, and you can do that within minutes. This will help you to control costs as well.

- **Developer productivity**: In a serverless model, your serverless vendor takes all the pain of setting up hardware, networking, and installing and managing software. Developers need to focus only on implementing the business logic and don't need to worry about underlying system engineering work, resulting in higher developer productivity.

- **No idle capacity**: With serverless models, you don't need to provision computing and storage capacity in advance. And you can scale up and down based on your application requirements. For example, if you have an e-commerce site, then you might need higher capacity during festive seasons than other days. So, you can just scale up resources for that period only.

  Moreover, today's serverless models, such as AWS, work on the "pay as you go" model, meaning that you don't pay for any capacity that you don't use. This way, you don't pay anything when your servers are idle, which helps to control costs.

- **Faster time to market**: With serverless models, you can start building software applications in minutes, as the infrastructure is ready to be used at any time. You can scale up or down underlying hardware in a few clicks. This saves you time with system engineering work and helps to launch applications much more quickly. This is one of the key factors for companies adopting the serverless model.

- **Deploy in minutes**: Today's serverless models simplify deployment by doing all the heavy lifting work and eliminating the need for managing any underlying infrastructure. These services follow DevOps practices.

## Introduction to AWS

AWS is a highly available, reliable, and scalable cloud service platform offered by Amazon that provides a broad set of infrastructure services. These services are delivered on an "on-demand" basis and are available in seconds. AWS was one of the first platforms to offer the "pay-as-you-go" pricing model, where there is no upfront expense. Rather, payment is made based on the usage of different AWS services. The AWS model provides users with compute, storage, and throughput as needed.

The AWS platform was first conceptualized in 2002 and **Simple Queue Service** (**SQS**) was the first AWS service, which was launched in 2004. However, the AWS concept has been reformulated over the years, and the AWS platform was officially relaunched in 2006, combining the three initial service offerings of Amazon S3 (**Simple Storage Service**): cloud storage, SQS, and EC2 (**Elastic Compute Cloud**). Over the years, AWS has become a platform for virtually every use case. From databases to deployment tools, from directories to content delivery, from networking to compute services, there are currently more than 100 different services available with AWS. More advanced features, such as machine learning, encryption, and big data are being developed at a rapid pace. Over the years, the AWS platform of products and services has become very popular with top enterprise customers. As per current estimates, over 1 million customers trust AWS for their IT infrastructure needs.

## AWS Serverless Ecosystem

We will take a quick tour of the AWS serverless ecosystem and briefly talk about the different services that are available. These services will be discussed in detail in future chapters.

Figure 1.4 shows the AWS serverless ecosystem, which is comprised of eight different AWS services:

- **Lambda**: AWS Lambda is a compute service that runs code in response to different events, such as in-app activity, website clicks, or outputs from connected devices, and automatically manages the compute resources required by the code. Lambda is a core component of the serverless environment and integrates with different AWS services to do the work that's required.

- **Simple Storage Service (S3)**: Amazon S3 is a storage service that you can use to store and retrieve any amount of information, at any time, from anywhere on the web. AWS S3 is a highly available and fault-tolerant storage service.

- **Simple Queue Service (SQS)**: Amazon SQS is a distributed message queuing service that supports message communication between computers over the internet. SQS enables an application to submit a message to a queue, which another application can then pick up at a later time.

- **Simple Notification Service (SNS)**: Amazon SNS is a notification service that coordinates the delivery of messages to subscribers. It works as a **publish/ subscribe** (**pub/sub**) form of asynchronous communication.

- **DynamoDB**: Amazon DynamoDB is a NoSQL database service.

- **Amazon Kinesis**: Amazon Kinesis is a real-time, fully managed, and scalable service.

- **Step Functions**: AWS Step Functions make it easy to coordinate components of distributed applications. Suppose you want to start running one component of your application after another one has completed successfully, or you want to run two components in parallel. You can easily coordinate these workflows using Step Functions. This saves you the time and effort required to build such workflows yourself and helps you to focus on business logic more.

- **Athena**: Amazon Athena is an interactive serverless query service that makes it easy to use standard SQL to analyze data in Amazon S3. It allows you to quickly query structured, unstructured, and semi-structured data that's stored in S3. With Athena, you don't need to load any datasets locally or write any complex **ETL** (**extract, transform, and load**), as it provides the capability to read data directly from S3. We will learn more about AWS Athena in *Chapter 4, Serverless Amazon Athena and the AWS Glue Data Catalog.*

Here's a diagram of the AWS serverless ecosystem:

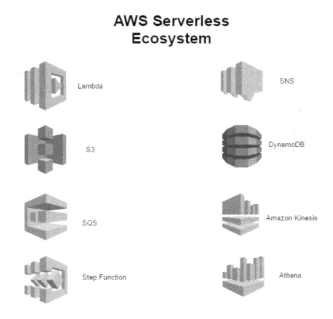

Figure 1.3 : The AWS serverless ecosystem Ecosystem

## AWS Lambda

AWS Lambda is a serverless computing platform that you can use to execute your code to build on-demand, smaller applications. It is a compute service that runs your backend code without you being involved in the provisioning or managing of any servers in the background.

The Lambda service scales automatically based on your usage and it has inbuilt fault-tolerance and high availability, so you don't need to worry about the implementation of HA or **DR** (**disaster recovery**) with AWS Lambda. You are only responsible for managing your code, so you can focus on the business logic and get your work done.

Once you upload your code to Lambda, the services handles all the capacity, scaling, patching, and infrastructure to run your code and provides performance visibility by publishing real-time metrics and logs to Amazon CloudWatch. You select the amount of memory allocation for your function (between 128 MB and 3 GB). Based on the amount of memory allocation, CPU and network resources are allocated to your function. You could also say that AWS Lambda is a function in code that allows stateless execution to be triggered by events. This also means that you cannot log in to actual compute instances or customize any underlying hardware.

With Lambda, you only pay for the time that your code is running. Once execution is completed, the Lambda service goes into idle mode and you don't pay for any idle time. AWS Lambda follows a very fine-grained pricing model, where you are charged for compute time in 100 ms increments. It also comes with a Free Tier, with which you can use Lambda for free until you reach a certain cap on the number of requests. We will study AWS Lambda pricing in more detail in a later section.

AWS Lambda is a great tool for triggering code in the cloud that functions based upon events. However, we need to remember that AWS Lambda (in itself) is stateless, meaning that your code should run as you develop it in a stateless manner. However, if required, a database such as DynamoDB can be used. Over the years, AWS Lambda has become very popular for multiple serverless use cases, such as web applications, data processing, IoT devices, voice-based applications, and infrastructure management.

## Supported Languages

Lambda is stateless and serverless. You should develop your code so that it runs in a stateless manner. If you want to use other third-party services or libraries, AWS allows you to zip up those folders and libraries and give them to Lambda in a ZIP file, which in turn enables other supportive languages that you would like to use.

AWS Lambda supports code written in the following six languages:

- Node.js (JavaScript)
- Python
- Java (Java 8 compatible)
- C# (.NET Core)
- Go
- PowerShell

> **Note**
>
> AWS Lambda could change the list of supported languages at any time. Check the AWS website for the latest information.

## Exercise 1: Running Your First Lambda Function

In this exercise, we'll create a Lambda function, specify the memory and timeout settings, and execute the function. We will create a basic Lambda function to generate a random number between 1 and 10.

Here are the steps for completion:

1. Open a browser and log in to the AWS console by going to this URL: https://aws. amazon.com/console/.

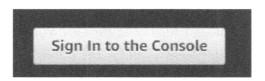

Figure 1.4 : The AWS console

2. Click on **Services** at the top-left of the page. Either look for **Lambda** in the listed services or type Lambda in the search box, and click on the **Lambda** service in the search result:

Figure 1.5 : AWS services

3. Click on **Create a function** to create your first Lambda function on the AWS Lambda page:

# Get started

Author a Lambda function from scratch, or choose from one of many preconfigured examples.

Figure 1.6 : The Get started window

4.  On the **Create function** page, select **Author from scratch**:

Create function

| Author from scratch | Blueprints | Serverless Application Repository |
|---|---|---|
| Start with a simple "hello world" example. | Choose a preconfigured template as a starting point for your Lambda function. | Find and deploy serverless apps published by developers, companies, and partners on AWS. |

Figure 1.7 : The Create function page

5.  In the **Author from scratch** window, fill in the following details:

**Name**: Enter `myFirstLambdaFunction`.

**Runtime**: Choose **Node.js 6.10**. The **Runtime** window dropdown shows the list of languages that are supported by AWS Lambda, and you can author your Lambda function code in any of the listed options. For this exercise, we will author our code in Node.js.

**Role**: Choose **Create new role from one or more template**. In this section, you specify an IAM role.

**Role name**: Enter `lambda_basic_execution`.

**Policy templates**: Select **Simple Microservice permissions**:

Figure 1.8 : The Author from scratch window

6. Now, click on **Create function**. You should see the message shown in the following screenshot:

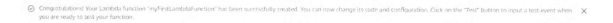

✓ Congratulations! Your Lambda function "myFirstLambdaFunction" has been successfully created. You can now change its code and configuration. Click on the "Test" button to input a test event when ✕ you are ready to test your function.

**Figure 1.9 : Output showing Lambda function creation**

So, you have created your first Lambda function, but we have yet to change its code and configuration based on our requirements. So, let's move on.

7. Go to the **Function code** section:

**Figure 1.10 : The Function code window**

8. Use the **Edit code inline** option to write a simple random number generator function.

9. The following is the required code for our sample Lambda function. We have declared two variables: **minnum** and **maxnum**. Then, we are using the **random()** method of the **Math** class to generate a random number. Finally, we call **"callback(null, generatednumber)"**. If an error occurs, null will be returned to the caller; otherwise, the value of the **generatednumber** variable will be passed as an output:

```
//TODO implement
    let minnum = 0;
    let maxnum = 10;
    let generatednumber = Math.floor(Math.random() * maxnum) + minnum
    callback(null, generatednumber);
```

10. In the **Basic settings** window, write `myLambdaFunction_settings` in the **Description** field, select **128 MB** in the **Memory** field, and have 3 sec in the **Timeout** field:

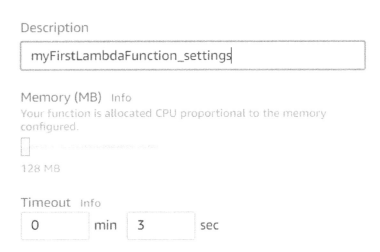

Figure 1.11 : The Basic settings window

11. That's it. Click on the **Save** button in the top-right corner of the screen. Congratulations! You have just created your first Lambda function:

Figure 1.12 : Output of the Lambda function created

12. Now, to run and test your function, you need to create a test event. This allows you to set up event data to be passed to your function. Click on the dropdown next to **Select a test event** in the top-right corner of the screen and select **Configure test event**:

Figure 1.13 : Lambda function Test window

13. When the popup appears, click on **Create new test event** and give it a name. Click on **Create** and the test event gets created:

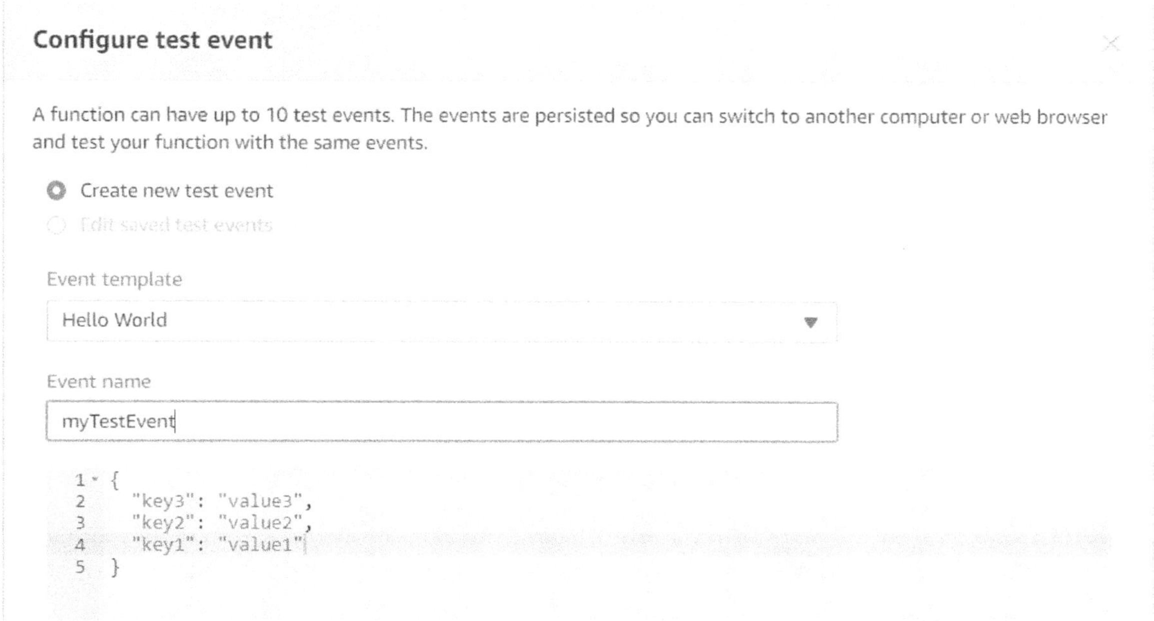

**Configure test event**                                                        ✕

A function can have up to 10 test events. The events are persisted so you can switch to another computer or web browser and test your function with the same events.

  ⦿  Create new test event
  ○  Edit saved test events

Event template

| Hello World ▼ |

Event name

| myTestEvent |

```
1 ▾ {
2      "key3": "value3",
3      "key2": "value2",
4      "key1": "value1"
5   }
```

**Figure 1.14 : The Configure test event window**

14. Click on the **Test** button next to test events and you should see the following window upon successful execution of the event:

⊘ Execution result: succeeded (logs)                                              ✕
  ▸ Details

**Figure 1.15 : The Test execution window**

15. Expand the **Details** tab and more details about the function execution appear, such as actual duration, billed duration, actual memory used, and configured memory:

Figure 1.16 : The Details tab

You don't need to manage any underlying infrastructure, such as EC2 instances or Auto Scaling groups. You only have to provide your code and let Lambda do the rest of the magic.

## Activity 1: Creating a New Lambda Function that Finds the Square Root of the Average of Two Input Numbers

Create a new Lambda function that finds the square root of the average of two input numbers. For example, the two numbers provided are 10 and 40. Their average is 25 and the square root of 25 is 5, so your result should be 5. This is a basic Lambda function that can be written using simple math functions.

Here are the steps for completion:

1. Follow the exercise that we just completed before this activity.

2. Go to the AWS Lambda service and create a new function.

3. Provide the function name, runtime, and role, as discussed in the previous exercise.

4. Under the section on **Function code**, write the code to find the square root of the average of two input numbers. Once done, save your code.

5. Create the test event and try to test the function by executing it.

6. Execute the function.

> **Note**
>
> The solution for this activity can be found on page 152.

## Limits of AWS Lambda

AWS Lambda imposes certain limits in terms of resource levels, according to your account level. Some notable limits imposed by AWS Lambda are as follows:

- **Memory Allocation**: You can allocate memory to your Lambda function with a minimum value of 128 MB and a maximum of 3,008 MB. Based on memory allocation, CPU and network resources are allocated to the Lambda function. So, if your Lambda function is resource-intensive, then you might like to allocate more memory to it. Needless to say, the cost of a Lambda function varies according to the amount of memory allocated to the function.

- **Execution Time**: Currently, the Lambda service caps the maximum execution time of your Lambda function at 15 minutes. If your function does not get completed by this time, it will be automatically be timed out.

- **Concurrent Executions**: The Lambda service allows up to 1000 total concurrent executions across all functions within a given region. Depending on your usage, you may want to set the concurrent execution limit for your functions, otherwise the overall costs may escalate very soon.

> **Note**
>
> If you want to learn more about other limits of Lambda functions, go to
> https://docs.aws.amazon.com/lambda/latest/dg/limits.html#limits-list.

## AWS Lambda Pricing Overview

AWS Lambda is a serverless compute service and you only pay for what you use, not for any idle time. There is a Free Tier associated with Lambda pricing. We will discuss the Lambda Free Tier in the next section.

To understand the AWS billing model for Lambda, you first need to understand the concept of GB-s.

1 GB-s is 1 Gigabyte of memory used per second. So, if your code uses 5 GB in 2 minutes, and then 3 GB in 3 minutes, the accumulated memory usage would be 5*120 + 3*180 = 1140 GB seconds.

> **Note**
>
> The prices for the AWS services discussed in this section and in this book are current at the time of writing, as AWS prices may change at any time. For the latest prices, please check the AWS website.

Lambda pricing depends on the following two factors:

- **Total Request Count**: This is the total number of times the Lambda function has been invoked to start executing in response to an event notification or invoke call. As part of the Free Tier, the first 1 million requests per month are free. There is a charge of $0.20 for 1 million requests beyond the limits of the Free Tier.

- **Total Execution Time**: This is the time taken from the start of your Lambda function execution until it either returns a value or terminates, rounded up to the nearest 100 ms. The price for execution time varies with the amount of memory allocated to your function. If you want to understand how the cost of total execution time varies with the total amount of memory allocated to the Lambda function, go to https://aws.amazon.com/lambda/pricing:

| Memory (MB) | Free tier seconds per month | Price per 100ms ($) |
| --- | --- | --- |
| 128 | 3,200,000 | 0.000000208 |
| 192 | 2,133,333 | 0.000000313 |
| 256 | 1,600,000 | 0.000000417 |
| 320 | 1,280,000 | 0.000000521 |
| 384 | 1,066,667 | 0.000000625 |
| 448 | 914,286 | 0.000000729 |
| 512 | 800,000 | 0.000000834 |
| 576 | 711,111 | 0.000000938 |
| 640 | 640,000 | 0.000001042 |
| 704 | 581,818 | 0.000001146 |
| 768 | 533,333 | 0.000001250 |

Figure 1.17 : Lambda pricing

## Lambda Free Tier

As part of the Lambda Free Tier, you can make 1 million free requests per month. You can have 400,000 GB-seconds of compute time per month. Since function duration costs vary with the allocated memory size, the memory size you choose for your Lambda functions determines how long they can run in the Free Tier.

> **Note**
>
> The Lambda Free Tier gets adjusted against monthly charges, and the Free Tier does not automatically expire at the end of your 12-month AWS Free Tier term, but is available to both existing and new AWS customers indefinitely.

## Activity 2: Calculating the Total Lambda Cost

We have a Lambda function that has 512 MB of memory allocated to it and there were 20 million calls for that function in a month, with each function call lasting 1 second. Calculate the total Lambda cost.

Here's how we calculate the cost:

1.  Note the monthly compute price and compute time provided by the Free Tier.

2.  Calculate the total compute time in seconds.

3.  Calculate the total compute time in GB-s.

4.  Calculate the monthly billable compute in GB- s. Here's the formula:

    *Monthly billable compute (GB- s) = Total compute – Free Tier compute*

5.  Calculate the monthly compute charges in dollars. Here's the formula:

    *Monthly compute charges = Monthly billable compute (GB-s) * Monthly compute price*

6.  Calculate the monthly billable requests. Here's the formula:

    *Monthly billable requests = Total requests – Free Tier requests*

7.  Calculate the monthly request charges. Here's the formula:

    *Monthly request charges = Monthly billable requests * Monthly request price*

8.  Calculate the total cost. Here's the formula:

    *Monthly compute charge + Monthly request charges*

> **Note**
>
> The solution for this activity can be found on page 153.

### Additional Costs

While estimating Lambda costs, you must be aware of additional costs. You will incur costs as part of Lambda integration with other AWS services such as DynamoDB or S3. For example, if you are using the Lambda function to read data from an S3 bucket and write output data into DynamoDB tables, you will incur additional charges for read from S3 and writing provisioned throughput to DynamoDB. We will study more about S3 and DynamoDB in *Chapter 2, Working with the AWS Serverless Platform.*

In summary, it may not seem like running Lambda functions costs a lot of money, but millions of requests and multiple functions per month tend to escalate the overall cost.

## Summary

In this chapter, we focused on understanding the serverless model and getting started with AWS and Lambda, the first building block of a serverless application on AWS. We looked at the main advantages and disadvantages of the serverless model and its use cases. We explained the serverless model, and worked with AWS serverless services. We also created and executed the AWS Lambda function.

In the next chapter, we'll look at the capabilities of the AWS Serverless Platform and how AWS supports enterprise-grade serverless applications, with and without Lambda. From Compute to API Gateway and from storage to databases, the chapter will cover the fully managed services that can be used to build and run serverless applications on AWS.

# Working with the AWS Serverless Platform

**Learning Objectives**

By the end of this chapter, you will be able to:

- Explain Amazon S3 and serverless deployments
- Use API Gateway and integrate it with AWS Lambda
- Work with fully managed services such as SNS, SQS, and DynamoDB

This chapter teaches you how to build and run serverless applications with AWS.

## Introduction

In the previous chapter, we focused on understanding the serverless model and getting started with AWS and Lambda, the first building blocks of a serverless application on AWS. You also learned about how the serverless model differs from traditional product development.

In this chapter, we will learn about other AWS capabilities such as S3, SNS, and SQS. You can start by asking students about different AWS serverless technologies that the students have heard about or have had the chance to work with. Talk to them briefly about different AWS services such as S3 storage, API Gateway, SNS, SQS, and DynamoDB services. We will discuss them in detail in this chapter.

## Amazon S3

Amazon Simple Storage Service or S3 is nothing but a cloud storage platform that lets you store and retrieve any amount of data anywhere. Amazon S3 provides unmatched durability, scalability, and availability so that you can store your data in one of the most secure ways. This storage service is accessible via simple web interfaces, which can either be REST or SOAP. Amazon S3 is one of the most supported platforms, so either you can use S3 as a standalone service or you can integrate it with other AWS services.

Amazon S3 is an object storage unit that stores data as objects within resources called "**buckets**". Buckets are containers for your objects and serve multiple purposes. Buckets let you organize Amazon namespaces at the highest level and also play a key role in access control. You can store any amount of objects within a bucket, while your object size can vary from 1 byte to 5 terabytes. You can perform read, write, and delete operations on your objects in the buckets.

Objects in S3 consist of metadata and data. Data is the content that you want to store in the object. Within a bucket, an object is uniquely identified by a key and a version ID. The key is the name of the object.

When you add a new object in S3, a version ID is generated and assigned to the object. Versioning allows you to maintain multiple versions of an object. Versioning in S3 needs to be enabled before you can use it.

> **Note**
>
> If versioning is disabled and you try to copy the object with the same name (key), it will overwrite the existing object.

A combination of bucket, key, and version ID allows you to uniquely identify each object in Amazon S3.

For example, if your bucket name is **aws-serverless** and the object name is **CreateS3Object.csv**, the following would be the fully qualified path of an object in S3:

**Figure 2.1: Fully qualified URL to access the aws-serverless bucket that has an object called CreateS3Object.csv**

## Key Characteristics of Amazon S3

Now, let's understand some of the key characteristics of using the Amazon S3 service:

- **Durability and high availability**: Amazon S3 provides durable infrastructure to store your data and promises a durability of Eleven 9s (99.999999999%). The Amazon S3 service is available in multiple regions around the world. Amazon S3 provides geographic redundancy within each region since your data gets copied automatically to at least three different availability zone locations within a region. Also, you have the option to replicate your data across regions. As we saw earlier, you can maintain multiple versions of your data as well, which can be used for recovery purposes later.

In the following diagram, you can see that when the S3 bucket in **source-region-A** goes down, **route 53** is redirected to the replicated copy in **source-region-B**:

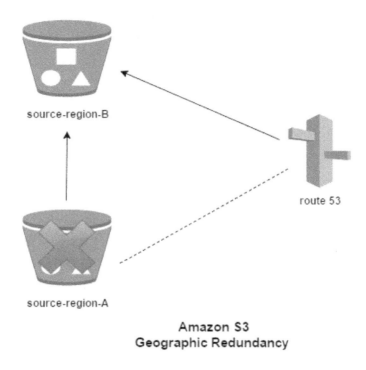

Figure 2.2: Amazon S3 Geographic Redundancy

> **Note**
>
> Geographic redundancy enables the replication of your data and stores this backup data in a separate physical location. You can always get your data back from this backup physical location just in case the main site fails.

- **Scalability**: Amazon S3 is a highly scalable service as it can scale up or scale down easily based on your business needs. Suppose, today, that you have an urgent need to run analytics on 500 GB of data and before you do analytics, you have to bring that data into the AWS ecosystem. Don't worry, as you can just create a new bucket and start uploading your data into it. All of the scalability work happens behind the scenes, without any impact on your business.

- **Security**: In Amazon S3, you can enable server-side encryption, which encrypts your data automatically while it is getting written on the S3 bucket. Data decryption happens by itself when someone wants to read the data. Amazon S3 also supports data transfer over SSL, and you can also configure bucket policies to manage object permissions and control access to your data using AWS **Identity and Access Management** (**IAM**). We will look at permissions in more detail in a later part of this chapter.

> **Note**
>
> Since it is server-side encryption, there is no user interference required. Hence, when a user tries to read the data, the server decrypts the data automatically.

- **Integration**: You can use Amazon S3 as a standalone service to store data or you can integrate it with other AWS services such as Lambda, Kinesis, and DynamoDB. We will look at some of these AWS services and their integration as part of our exercises in a later part of this chapter.

- **Low cost**: Like other AWS serverless services, Amazon S3 works on a pay-as-you-go model. This means that there are no upfront payments and you pay based on your usage. Since it is a serverless offering, you don't need to manage any underlying hardware or network resources. Therefore, there is no need to buy and manage expensive hardware. This helps to keep costs low with Amazon S3.

- **Access via APIs**: You can use the REST API to make requests to Amazon S3 endpoints.

## Deploying a Static Website

With Amazon S3, you can host your entire static website at a low cost, while leveraging a highly available and scalable hosting solution to meet varied traffic demands.

## Exercise 2: Setting up a Static Website with an S3 Bucket Using a Domain Name in Route 53

In this exercise, we'll look at doing the following:

- Creating an S3 bucket and providing required permissions
- Uploading a file onto an S3 bucket, which will be used to set the default page of your website
- Configuring your S3 bucket

So, let's get started. Here are the steps to perform this exercise:

1. Log in to your AWS account using your credentials.

2. Click on the dropdown next to **Services** on top-left side and type **S3**:

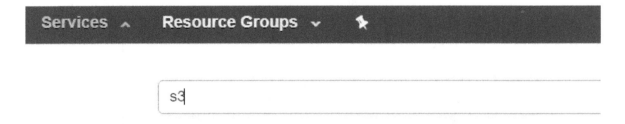

Figure 2.3: Searching Amazon S3 services via the dropdown option

3. The Amazon S3 page will open. Click on **Create Bucket**:

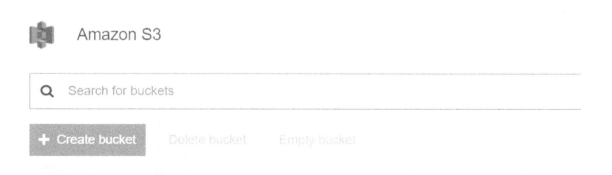

Figure 2.4: Creating an Amazon S3 bucket

4.  The **Create bucket** dialog box will open. You need to provide the following information:

    **Bucket Name**: Enter a unique bucket name. For this book, we've used `www.aws-serverless.tk` since we will host a website using our S3 bucket. As per AWS guidelines, a bucket name must be unique across all existing bucket names in Amazon S3. So, you need to choose your individual bucket names.

    **Region**: Click on the dropdown next to **Region** and select the region where you want to create the bucket. We will go with the default region, **US-East (N. Virginia)**.

    If you want to copy these settings from any other bucket and want to apply them to the new bucket, you can click on the dropdown next to **Copy settings from an existing bucket**. We will configure the settings for this bucket here, so we will leave this option blank:

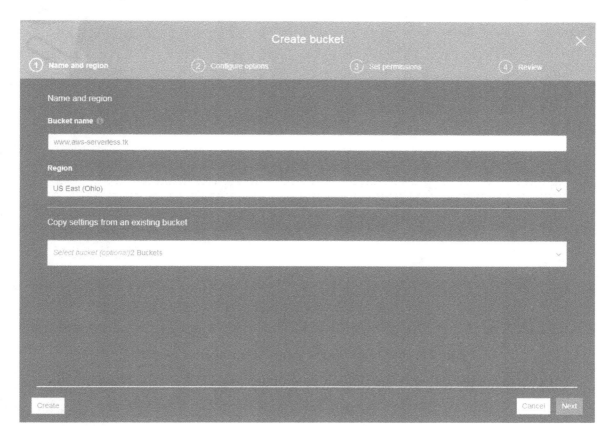

Figure 2.5: The Create bucket menu: Name and region section

5.  Click on **Next**. We will be taken to the **Properties** window. Here, we can set the following properties of the S3 bucket:

**Versioning**

**Server access logging**

**Tags**

**Object-level logging**

**Default encryption**

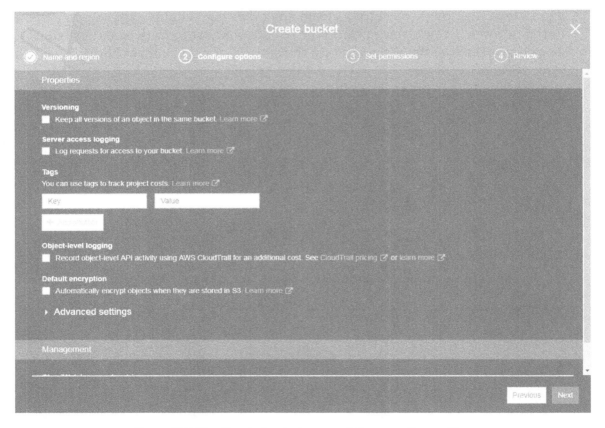

Figure 2.6: The Create bucket menu: Set properties section

For this exercise, go with the default properties and click on the **Next** button.

6. The next window is **Set permissions**. Here, we grant read and write permissions for this bucket to other AWS users and manage public permissions as well. We can see in the following screenshot that the owner of the bucket has both read and write permissions by default. If you want to give permission for this bucket to any other AWS account as well, you can click on **Add Account**:

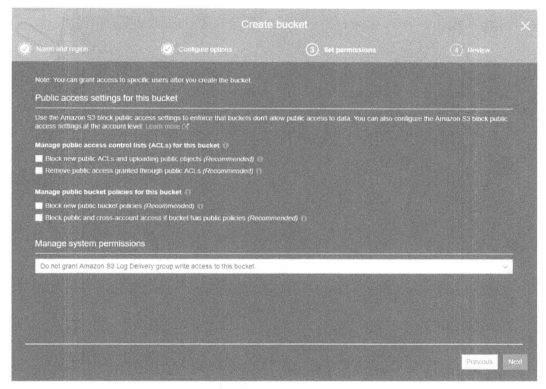

Figure 2.7: The Create bucket menu: Set permissions option

7. Keep all of the checkboxes unchecked. We'll host a website using this S3 bucket.

8. Keep **Manage system permissions** with the default settings and click on the **Next** button to go to the **Review** screen. Here, you can review all of the settings for your S3 bucket. If you want to change anything, click on the **Edit** button and change it. Alternatively, click on **Create Bucket** and your bucket will be created:

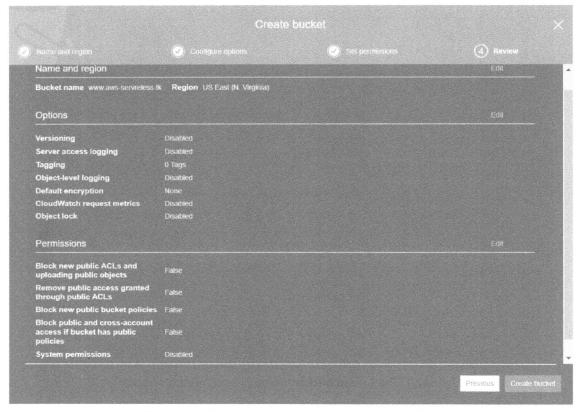

Figure 2.8: The Create bucket menu: Review section

9. Click on the newly created bucket name and click on the second tab, **Properties**, and enable **Static website hosting**:

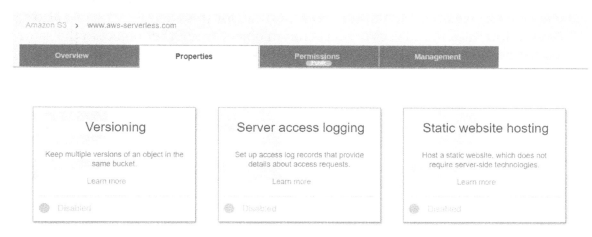

Figure 2.9: Enabling the Static website hosting option under the Properties section

10. Select the **Use this bucket to host a website** option. Enter the name of the index document. This document will be used to display the home page of your website. You can also add an **error.html** file, which will be used to display the page in case of any error. We aren't adding an **error.html** file for this exercise. You can also set redirection rules to redirect requests for an object to another object in the same bucket or to an external URL. Click on the **Save** button to save it:

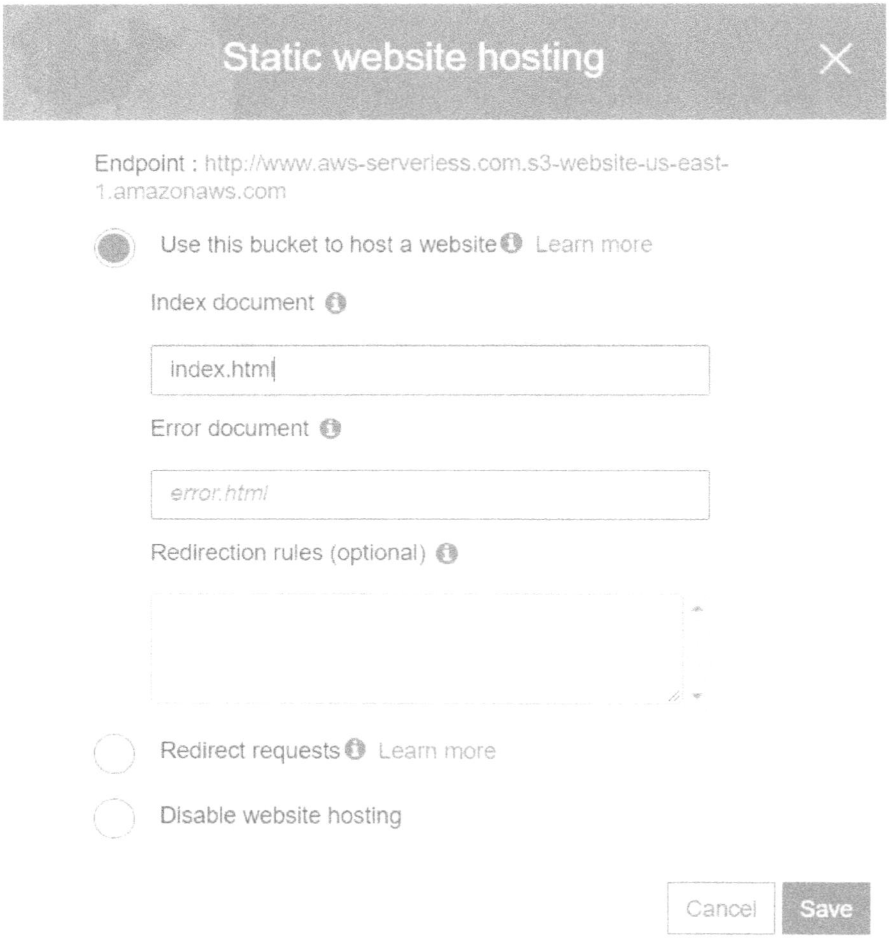

**Figure 2.10: The Static website hosting menu**

---

**Note**

At the top, note the **Endpoint** information. This will be the URL to access your website. In this case, it is **http://www.aws-serverless.com.s3-website-us-east-1.amazonaws.com/**.

11. Next, click on the **Overview** tab.

12. In the **Overview** tab, click on **Upload**. Click on **Add files**. Upload the `index.html` page (found in the `Chapter02` folder of the code bundle) as an object into our S3 bucket. Now, click on the **Next** button:

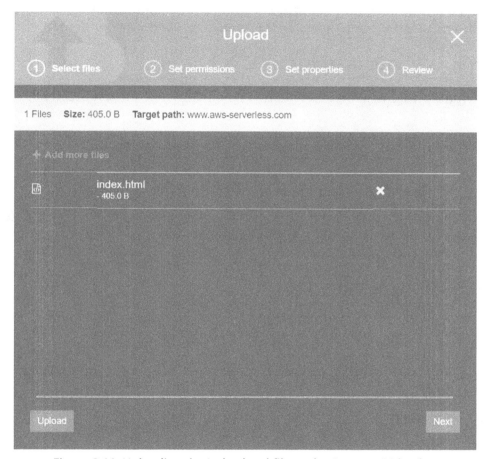

Figure 2.11: Uploading the Index.html file to the Amazon S3 bucket

> **Note**
>
> The `index.html` file is a simple HTML file that contains basic tags, which are for demonstration purposes only.

13. Under **Manage Public Permissions**, select **Grant public read access to this object(s)**. Keep the rest of the settings as they are.

14. Click on **Next**. Keep all of the properties to their default values on the **Set properties** screen. On the next screen, review the object properties and click on the **Upload** button.

    Congratulations! You have just deployed your website using the Amazon S3 bucket.

15. Go to a browser on your machine and go to the endpoint that we noted in step 10. You should see the home page (`index.html`) displayed on your screen:

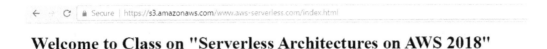

Secure | https://s3.amazonaws.com/www.aws-serverless.com/index.html
Welcome to Class on "Serverless Architectures on AWS 2018"
We are deploying a static website with a serverless architecture here!!

Figure 2.12: Viewing the uploaded Index.html file on the browser

We have successfully deployed our S3 bucket as a static website. There are different use case scenarios for S3 services, such as media hosting, backup and storage, application hosting, software, and data delivery.

## Enabling Versioning on S3 Bucket

Now, we'll look at enabling versioning on an S3 bucket. Here are the steps to do so:

1. Log in to your AWS account.
2. In the S3 bucket name list, choose the name of the bucket that you want to enable versioning for.
3. Select **Properties**.
4. Select **Versioning**.
5. Choose **Enable versioning or Suspend versioning** and then click on **Save**.

## S3 and Lambda Integration

Your Lambda function can be called using Amazon S3. Here, the event data is passed as a parameter. This integration enables you to write Lambda functions that process Amazon S3 events, for example, when a new S3 bucket gets created and you want to take an action. You can write a Lambda function and invoke it based on the activity from Amazon S3:

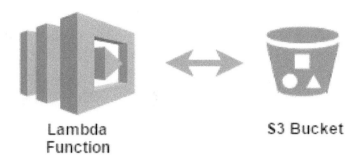

**Figure 2.13: Demonstrating the integration of AWS S3 with AWS Lambda**

### Exercise 3: Writing a Lambda Function to Read a Text File

In this exercise, we will demonstrate AWS S3 integration with the AWS Lambda service. We will create an S3 bucket and load a text file. Then, we will write a Lambda function to read that text file. You will see an enhancement for this demonstration later in this chapter when we integrate it further with the API Gateway service to show the output of that text file as an API response.

Here are the steps to perform this exercise:

1. Go to the AWS services console and open the S3 dashboard. Click on **Create bucket** and provide a bucket name. Let's call it `lambda-s3-demo`. Note that your bucket name must be unique:

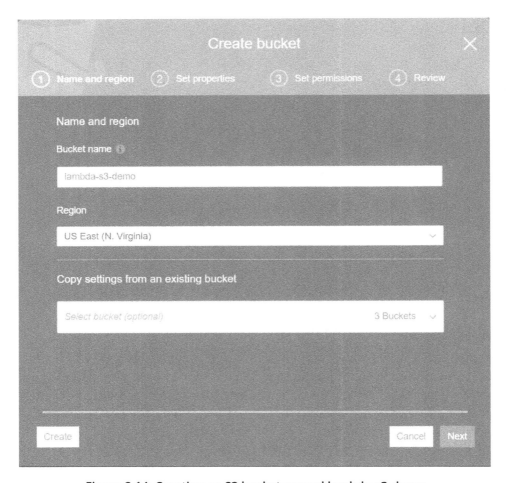

Figure 2.14: Creating an S3 bucket named lambda-s3-demo

2. Click on **Next** and follow the instructions to create the bucket. Set all of the settings as default. Since we will write the Lambda function using the same account, we don't need to provide any explicit permission to this bucket.

3. Create a file in your local disk and add the content `Welcome to Lambda and S3 integration demo Class!!` in the file. Save it as `sample.txt`.

4. Drag and drop this file into the **Upload** window to upload it to the newly created S3 bucket.

5. Click on **Upload**:

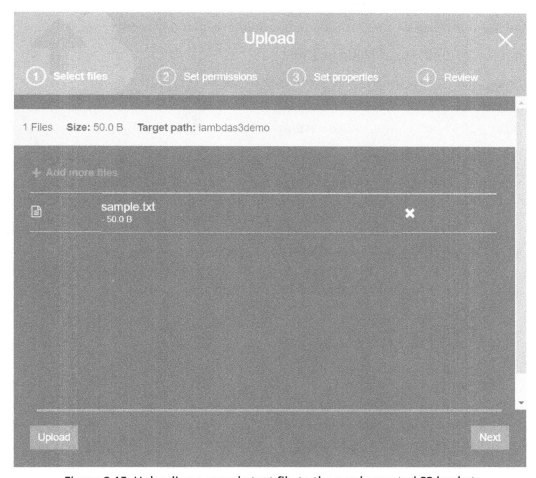

Figure 2.15: Uploading a sample text file to the newly created S3 bucket

Note

Observe the contents of this file's text message: **Welcome to Lambda and S3 integration demo Class!!**.

6. Go to the AWS service portal, search for Lambda, and open the Lambda dashboard. Click on **Create function** and provide the following details:

   Provide the name of the Lambda function. Let's name it **read_from_s3**.

   Choose the runtime as **Node.js 6.10**.

   Choose the **Create a new role from one or more templates** option. Provide the role name as **read_from_s3_role**.

   Under policy templates, choose **Amazon S3 object read-only permissions**.

7. Click on **Create function**.

8. Once the Lambda function has been created, jump to the **Function code** section and replace the contents of the **index.js** file with the following code and save it. You can also copy this code from the **s3_with_lambda.js** file. In this script, we are creating two variables, **src_bkt** and **src_key**, which will contain the name of the S3 bucket and the name of the file that was uploaded to the bucket. Then, we will retrieve that file as an object from the S3 bucket using **s3.getObject** and return the contents of the file as an output of the Lambda function:

```
var AWS = require('aws-sdk');
var s3 = new AWS.S3();

exports.handler = function(event, context, callback) {

    // Create variables the bucket & key for the uploaded S3 object
    var src_bkt = 'lambdas3demo';
    var src_key = 'sample.txt';

    // Retrieve the object
    s3.getObject({
        Bucket: src_bkt,
        Key: src_key
    }, function(err, data) {
        if (err) {
            console.log(err, err.stack);
            callback(err);
        }
```

```
else {
        console.log('\n\n' + data.Body.toString()+'\n');
        callback(null, data.Body.toString());
    }
});
};
```

Note that the default output of the data will be in binary format, so we are using the **toString** function to convert that binary output to a string:

```
index.js                 x

6     //Create variables the bucket & key for the uploaded S3 object
7     var src_bkt = 'lambdas3demo';
8     var src_key = 'sample.txt';
9
10    // Retrieve the object
11    s3.getObject({
12        Bucket: src_bkt,
13        Key: src_key
14    }, function(err, data) {
15        if (err) {
16            console.log(err, err.stack);
17            callback(err);
18        } else {
19            console.log('\n\n' + data.Body.toString()+'\n');
20            callback(null, data.Body.toString());
21        }
```

Figure 2.16: Illustrating the use of the toString() function

9. Click on the **Save** button to save the Lambda function.

10. Test the function now. But, before you can test it, you will have to configure test events, like we have done in earlier exercises. Once a test event is configured, click on **Test** to execute the Lambda function.

Once the function has been executed, you should see the highlighted message **Welcome to Lambda and S3 integration demo Class !!**, as provided in the following screenshot. This message was the content of the `sample.txt` file that we uploaded into our S3 bucket in step 3:

Figure 2.17: Demonstrating the Lambda function's execution

Now, we have completed our discussion about S3 integration with a Lambda function.

## API Gateway

API development is a complex process, and is a process that is constantly changing. As part of API development, there are many inherent complex tasks, such as managing multiple API versions, implementation of access and authorization, managing underlying servers, and doing operational work. All of this makes API development more challenging and impactful on an organization's ability to deliver software in a timely, reliable, and repeatable way.

**Amazon API Gateway** is a service from Amazon that takes care of all API development-related issues (discussed previously) and enables you to make your API development process more robust and reliable. Let's look into this in more detail now.

## What is API Gateway?

Amazon API Gateway is a fully managed service that focuses on creating, publishing, maintaining, monitoring, and securing APIs. Using API Gateway, you can create an API that acts as a single point of integration for external applications while you implement business logic and other required functionality at the backend using other AWS services.

With API Gateway, you can define your REST APIs with a few clicks in an easy-to-use GUI environment. You can also define API endpoints, their associated resources and methods, manage authentication and authorization for API consumers, manage incoming traffic to your backend systems, maintain multiple versions of the same API, and perform operational monitoring of API metrics as well. You can also leverage the managed cache layer, where the API Gateway service stores API responses, resulting in faster response times.

The following are the major benefits of using API Gateway. We have seen similar benefits of using other AWS services, such as Lambda and S3:

- Scalability
- Operational monitoring
- Pay-as-you-go model
- Security
- Integration with other AWS services

## API Gateway Concepts

Let's understand certain concepts of the API Gateway and how they work. This will help you build a better understanding on how the API Gateway works:

- **API endpoints**: An API endpoint is one end of the communication, a location from where the API can access all the required resources.
- **Integration requests**: The integration request specifies how your frontend will communicate with the backend system. Also, requests may need to be transformed based on the type of backend system running. Possible integration types are Lambda, AWS service, HTTP, and Mock.

- **Integration response**: After the backend system processes the requests, API Gateway consumes it. Here, you specify how the errors/response codes received from backend systems are mapped to the ones defined in API gateway.

- **Method request**: The method request is a contract between the user (public interface) and the frontend system on what will be the request mode. This includes the API authorization and HTTP definitions.

- **Method response**: Similar to the API method request, you can specify the method response. Here, you can specify the supported HTTP status codes and header information.

## Exercise 4: Creating a REST API and Integrating It with Lambda

Now, we will look at a demo of API Gateway and explore its different features. Along with this demo, we will also create a simple REST API using API Gateway and integrate it with a Lambda function. We will extend our earlier exercise on S3 integration with Lambda and create a REST API to show the contents of "`sample.txt`" as API response. This API will be integrated with Lambda to execute the function, and a **GET** method will be defined to capture the contents of the file and show it as the API response:

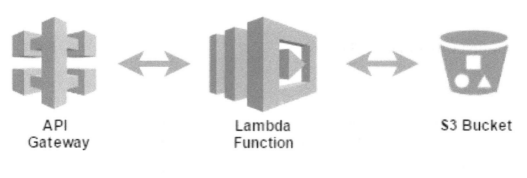

API
Gateway                     Lambda                   S3 Bucket
                            Function

API Gateway &
Lambda Integration

Figure 2.18: Illustrating the various feature integrations of API Gateway
with Lambda functions

Here are the steps to perform this exercise:

1.  Open a browser and log in to the AWS console: https://aws.amazon.com/console/.

2.  Click on the dropdown next to **Services** or type `API Gateway` in the search box and click on the service:

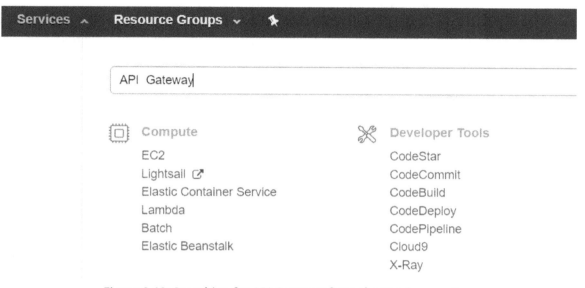

Figure 2.19: Searching for API Gateway from the Services section

3. On the API Gateway dashboard, if you're visiting the page for the first time, click on **Get Started**. Otherwise, you will see the following **Create New API** screen:

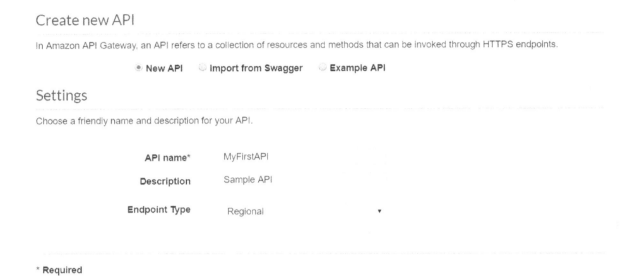

Figure 2.20: The Create new API page

Here, you have three options for choose from:

**New API**

**Import from Swagger**

**Example API**

4. Select **New API** and provide the following details:

**API name**: Enter `read_from_S3_api`

**Description**: Enter `sample API`

**Endpoint Type**: Choose **Regional** and click on **Create API**.

Figure 2.21: Creating a new API with the specified details

5. On the next page, click on **Actions**. You will see some options listed as **Resources** and **Methods**. A resource works as a building block for any RESTful API and helps in abstracting the information. Methods define the kind of operation to be carried out on the resources. A resource has a set of methods that operate on it, such as **GET**, **POST**, and **PUT**.

   We haven't created any resources yet as part of this exercise, so the AWS console will only have the root resource and no other resources.

6. Now, create a resource. On the resource dashboard, provide the resource name and click on **Create Resource** from the dropdown of **Action**.

7. Type `read_file_from_s3` in the **Resource Name** field and click on **Create Resource**:

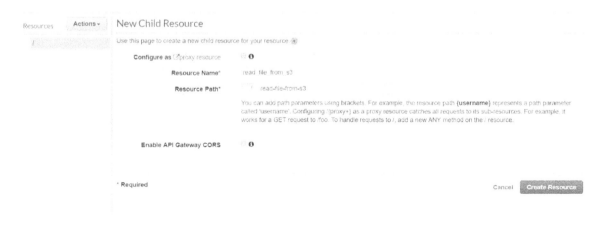

Figure 2.22: Creating a resource with the provided information

8. Create a method to access the information. Select that resource and then click on **Actions** to create a method. Choose **GET** from the available methods and click on ✓ to confirm the **GET** method type:

**Figure 2.23: Creating a method to access the available information**

9. Now, choose **Lambda Function** as the integration type:

**Figure 2.24: Selecting Lambda Function as an integration type**

10. Once you click on **Save**, you will get following warning. Here, AWS is asking you to provide API Gateway permission to invoke the Lambda function:

**Figure 2.25: Warning notification to enable API Gateway's permission**

11. Click on the **OK** button. The following screen will appear, which shows the workflow of the API. The following are the steps taken by the API:

Your API will invoke the Lambda function.

The Lambda function gets executed and sends the response back to the API.

The API receives the response and publishes it:

Figure 2.26: Illustrating the workflow of an API

12. Now, it's time to deploy the API. Click on the **Actions** dropdown and select **Deploy API**:

Figure 2.27: The Deploy API menu

13. Create a new deployment stage. Let's call it **prod**. Then, click on **Deploy** to deploy your API:

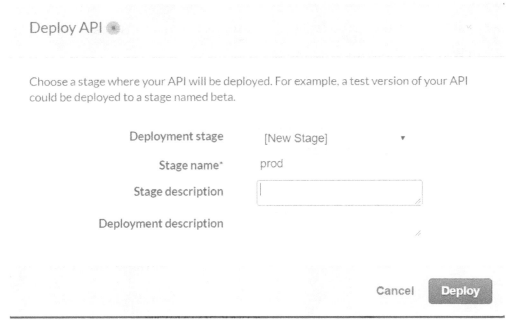

Figure 2.28: Creating a new deployment stage named prod

14. Once the API has been deployed, you should see the following screen. This screen has a few advanced settings so that you can configure your API. Let's skip this:

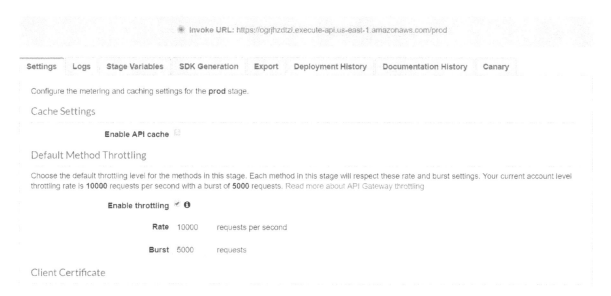

Figure 2.29: The menu options of the deployed API

15. Click on **prod** to open the submenu and select the **GET** method that you created for the API. Invoke the API URL that appears on the screen. You can access this link to access your API:

Figure 2.30: Invoking the API URL

This is what will appear on your screen:

```
C    🔒 Secure | https://ogrjhzdtzi.execute-api.us-east-1.amazonaws.com/prod/read-from-s3

// 20180419154045
// https://ogrjhzdtzi.execute-api.us-east-1.amazonaws.com/prod/read-from-s3


"Welcome to Lambda and S3 integration demo Class !!"
```

Figure 2.31: Illustrating the web page of the invoked URL

Great! You have just integrated the API Gateway with Lambda and S3.

# Other Native Services

We'll now turn our focus to other native services. We'll begin with Amazon SNS and then move on to Amazon SQS.

### Amazon SNS

Amazon **Simple Notification Services** (**SNS**) is the cloud-based notification service that's provided by AWS that enables the delivery of messages to the recipients or to the devices. SNS uses the publisher/subscriber model for the delivery of messages. Recipients can either subscribe to one or more "topics" within SNS or can be subscribed by the owner of a particular topic. AWS SNS supports message deliveries over multiple transport protocols.

AWS SNS is very easy to set up and can scale very well depending on the number of messages. Using SNS, you can send messages to a large number of subscribers, especially mobile devices. For example, let's say you have set up the monitoring for one of your RDS instances in AWS, and once the CPU goes beyond 80%, you want to send an alert in the form of an email. You can set up an SNS service to achieve this notification goal:

Figure 2.32: Establishing the alert mechanism using the SNS services

You can set up AWS SNS using the AWS Management Console, AWS command-line interface, or using the AWS SDK. You can use Amazon SNS to broadcast messages to other AWS services such as AWS Lambda, Amazon SQS, and to HTTP endpoints, email, or SMS as well.

Let's quickly understand the basic components, along with their functions, of Amazon SNS:

- **Topic**: A topic is a communication channel that is used to publish messages. Alternatively, you can subscribe to a topic to start receiving messages. It provides a communication endpoint for publishers and subscribers to talk to each other.

- **Publication of messages**: Amazon SNS allows you to publish messages that are then delivered to all the endpoints that have been configured as subscribers for a particular topic.

Here are some of the applications of Amazon SNS:

- **Subscription to messages**: Using SNS, you can subscribe to a particular topic and start receiving all the messages that get published to that particular topic.

- **Endpoints**: With Amazon SNS, you publish messages to the endpoints, which can be different applications based on your needs. You can have an HTTP endpoint, or you can deliver your messages to other AWS services (as endpoints) such as SQS and Lambda. Using SNS, you can configure emails or mobile SMS as possible endpoints as well. Please note that the mobile SMS facility is available in limited countries. Please check the Amazon SNS documentation for more details.

## Amazon SQS

In a simple message queue service, we have applications playing the roles of producers and consumers. The applications, known as producers, create messages and deliver them to the queues. Then, there is another application, called the consumer, which connects to the queue and receives the messages. Amazon SQL is a managed service adaptation of such message queue services.

Amazon **Simple Queue Service** (**SQS**) is a fully managed messaging queue service that enables applications to communicate by sending messages to each other:

SQS
Message Queue

Figure 2.33: Enabling Amazon SQS for better communication between applications

Amazon SQS provides a secure, reliable way to set up message queues. Currently, Amazon SQS supports two types of message queues:

- **Standard queues**: Standard queues can support close to unlimited throughput, that is, an unlimited number of transactions per second. These queues don't enforce the ordering of messages, which means that messages may be delivered in a different order than they were originally sent. Also, standard queues work on the **at-least-once** model, in which messages are delivered at least once, but they may be delivered more than once as well. Therefore, you need to have a mechanism in place to handle message duplication. You should use standard queues, whose throughput is more important than the order of requests.

- **FIFO queues**: FIFO queues work on the **First-In-First-Out** message delivery model, wherein the ordering of messages is maintained. Messages are received in the same order in which they were sent. Due to ordering and other limitations, FIFO queues don't have the same throughput as what's provided by standard queues. Note that FIFO queues are available in limited AWS regions. Please check the AWS website for more details. You should use FIFO queues when the order of messages is important.

> **Note**
>
> There is a limit on the number of messages supported by FIFO queues.

- **Dead Letter (DL) queues**: DL queues are queues that can receive messages that can't be processed successfully. You can configure a dead letter queue as a target for all unprocessed messages from other queues.

Just like Amazon SNS, you can also set up the AWS SQS service using the AWS Management Console, AWS command-line interface, or using the AWS SDK.

## DynamoDB

Amazon DynamoDB is a NoSQL database service that is fully managed. Here, you won't have to face the operative and scaling challenges of a distributed database. Like other serverless AWS services, with DynamoDB, you don't have to worry about hardware provisioning setup, configuration data replication, or cluster scaling.

DynamoDB uses the concept of partition keys to spread data across partitions for scalability, so it's important to choose an attribute with a wide range of values and that is likely to have evenly distributed access patterns.

With DynamoDB, you pay only for the resources you provision. There is no minimum fee or upfront payment required to use DynamoDB. The pricing of DynamoDB depends on the provisioned throughput capacity.

## Throughput Capacity

In DynamoDB, when you plan to provision a table, how do you know the throughput capacity required to get optimal performance out of your application?

The amount of capacity that you provision depends on how many reads you are trying to execute per second, and also how many write operations you are trying to do per second. Also, you need to understand the concept of strong and eventual consistency. Based on your settings, DynamoDB will reserve and allocate enough Amazon resources to keep low response times and partition data over enough servers to meet the required capacity to keep the application's read and write requirements.

> **Note**
>
> Eventual consistency is a type of consistency where there is no guarantee that what you are reading is the latest updated data. Strong consistency is another type of consistency where you always read the most recent version of the data. Eventual consistent operations consume half of the capacity of strongly consistent operations.

Now, let's look at some important terms:

- **Read capacity**: How many items you expect to read per second. You also have to specify the item size of your request. Two kilobyte items consume twice the throughput of one kilobyte items.

- **Write capacity**: How many items you expect to write per second.

> **Note**
>
> You are charged for reserving these resources, even if you don't load any data into DynamoDB. You can always change the provisioned read and write values later.

## DynamoDB Streams

DynamoDB Streams is a service that helps you capture table activity for DynamoDB tables. These streams provide an ordered sequence of item-level modifications in a DynamoDB table and store the information for up to 24 hours. You can combine DynamoDB Streams with other AWS services to solve different kinds of problems, such as audit logs, data replication, and more. DynamoDB Streams ensure the following two things:

- No duplicity of stream records, which ensures that each stream record will only appear once

- The ordered sequence of streams is maintained, which means that stream records appear in the same sequence as the modifications to the table

AWS maintains separate endpoints for DynamoDB and DynamoDB Streams. To work with database tables and indexes, your application must access a DynamoDB endpoint. To read and process DynamoDB Stream records, your application must access a DynamoDB Streams endpoint in the same region.

## DynamoDB Streams Integration with Lambda

Amazon DynamoDB is integrated with AWS Lambda. This enables you to create triggers that can respond to events automatically in DynamoDB Streams. With triggers, you can build applications that react to data modifications in DynamoDB tables.

Integration with Lambda allows you to perform many different actions with DynamoDB Streams, such as storing data modifications on S3 or sending notifications using AWS services such as SNS.

## Exercise 5: Creating an SNS topic and Subscribing to It

In this exercise, we'll create an SNS topic and subscribe to it. So, let's get started:

1. Go to AWS services and type **SNS** in the search box. Once you click on **Simple Notification Service (SNS)**, the following screen will appear. Click on **Get started**, which will take you to the SNS dashboard:

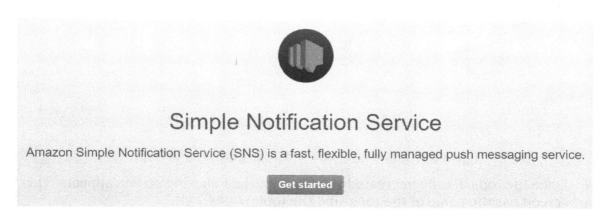

Figure 2.34: Creating a new SNS service

2. Click on **Topics** on the left menu and click on **Create new topic**:

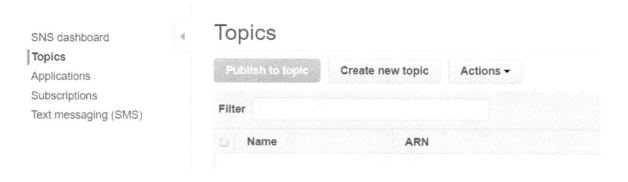

Figure 2.35: Creating a new topic from the Topics section

3. Provide the **Topic name** as **TestSNS** and the **Display name** as **TestSNS**, and click on **Create topic**. The **Topic name** and **Display name** can be different as well:

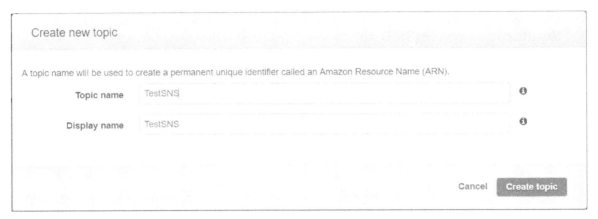

Figure 2.36: Providing a Topic and Display name for the topic

4. Once the topic has been created successfully, the following screen appears. This screen has the name of the topic and the topic's ARN.

> **Note**
> ARN stands for Amazon Resource Name, and it is used to identify a particular resource in AWS.

Figure 2.37: Summary page of the newly created topic

Note that if you need to reference a particular AWS resource in any other AWS service, you do so using the ARN.

We have successfully created a topic. Let's go ahead and create a subscription for this topic. We will set up an email notification as part of the subscription creation so that whenever something gets published to the topic, we will get an email notification.

5. Click on **Subscriptions** on the left menu and then click on **Create subscription**:

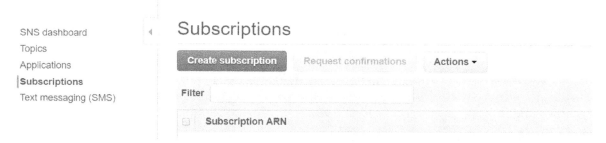

**Figure 2.38: Creating a subscription for the SNS service**

6. Provide the ARN for the topic that we created in step 4. Click on the dropdown next to **Protocol** and choose **Email**. Provide an email address as a value for the endpoint. Then, click on **Create subscription**:

| Create subscription | |
| --- | --- |
| Topic ARN | arn:aws:sns:us-east-1:989301460252:TestSNS |
| Protocol | Email |
| Endpoint | user@example.com |

Cancel  **Create subscription**

**Figure 2.39: Providing details to create a new subscription**

7.  Once the subscription has been created successfully, you should see the following screenshot. Note that the current status of the subscription is **PendingConfirmation**:

**Figure 2.40: The summary of the newly created subscription**

8.  Check your emails. You should have received an email notification from Amazon to confirm the subscription. Click on **Confirm Subscription**:

**Figure 2.41: Verifying the subscription from the registered email address**

Once the subscription is confirmed, you should see the following screenshot:

**Figure 2.42: The Subscription confirmed message**

9. Now, go back to the **Subscription** page and you will notice that **PendingConfirmation** is gone. Click on the refresh button if you still see **PendingConfirmation**. It should now be gone:

Figure 2.43: Summary of the confirmed ARN subscription

So, you have successfully created an SNS topic and have successfully subscribed to that topic as well. Whenever anything gets published to this topic, you will get an email notification.

## Exercise 6: SNS Integration with S3 and Lambda

In this exercise, we will see create a Lambda function and integrate it with SNS to send email notifications:

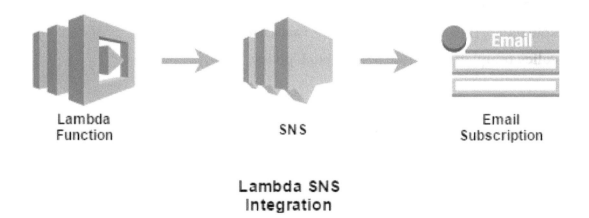

Figure 2.44: Integrating a Lambda function with SNS to enable an email subscription

Here are the steps to perform this exercise:

1. Go to the AWS service console and type **Lambda** in the search box. Then, open the Lambda management page.

2. Click on **Create function** and continue with the current selection, that is, **Author from scratch**:

Figure 2.45: Creating a Lambda function from scratch

3. Now, provide the following details:

**Name**: Write `lambda_with_sns`.

**Runtime**: Keep it as Node.js.

**Role**: Select **Create role from template** from the dropdown. Here, we are creating a Lambda function to send an SNS notification.

**Role name**: Provide the role name as `LambdaSNSRole`.

**Policy templates**: Choose **SNS publish policy**:

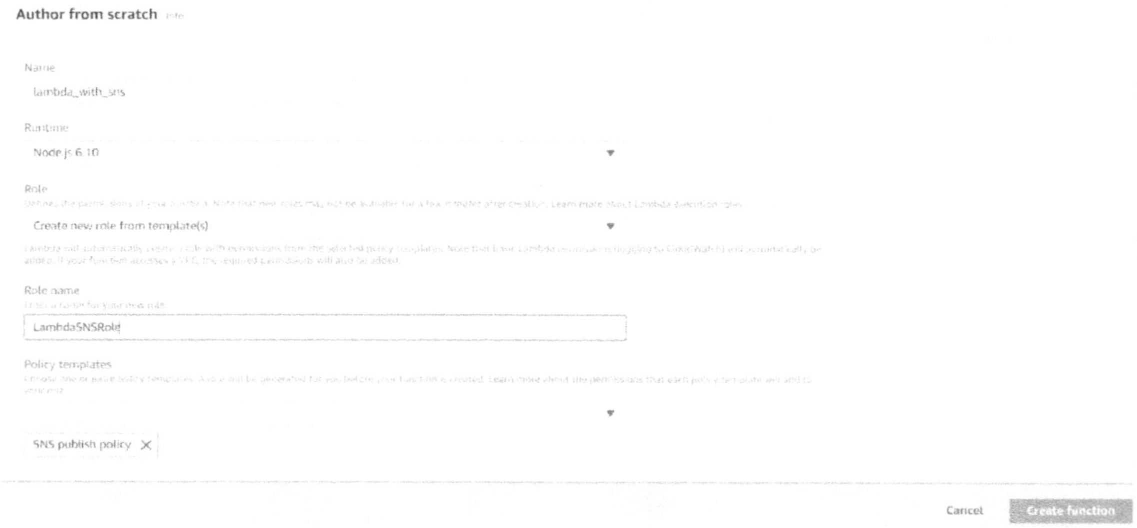

Figure 2.46: The menu options to create a Lambda function from scratch

4. Now, click on **Create function**. Once the function has been created successfully, you should see the following message:

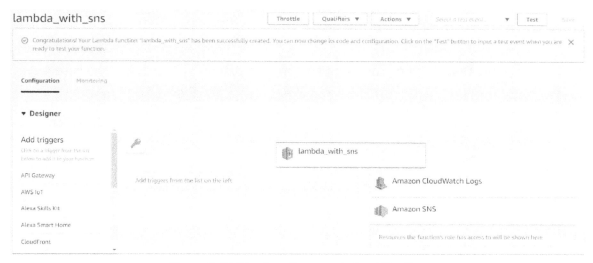

Figure 2.47: The function created notification

5. Let's jump to the function's code section. Go to the Git project and copy and paste the code in the code section of this page:

```javascript
var aws_sdk = require('aws-sdk');
aws_sdk.config.region = 'us-east-1';

exports.handler = function(event, context) {
    var sns = new aws_sdk.SNS();

    sns.publish({
        Message: 'Publish Test Message to SNS from Lambda',
        TopicArn: 'arn:aws:sns:us-east-1:989301460252:TestSNS'
    }, function(err, data) {
        if (err) {
            console.log(err.stack);
            return;
        }
        console.log('Message sent successfully');
        console.log(data);
```

Figure 2.48: Adding code from the Git project to the code section of the function

The following is an explanation of the main parts of the code:

**sns.publish:** The publish action is used to send a message to an Amazon SNS topic. In our case, we have an email subscription on the topic, we are trying to publish onto. Therefore, a successful publishing here will result in an email notification.

**Message:** The message you want to send to the topic. This message text will be delivered to the subscriber.

**TopicArn:** The topic you want to publish to. Here, we are publishing to the "TestSNS" topic, which we created in our previous exercise. So, copy and paste the ARN of the topic that we created in the earlier exercise here.

6.  Click on the **Save** button on the top right corner. Now, we are ready to test the code.

7.  Click on the **Test** button. You need to configure the test event. Let's create a test event with the name **TestEvent** and click on the **Save** button:

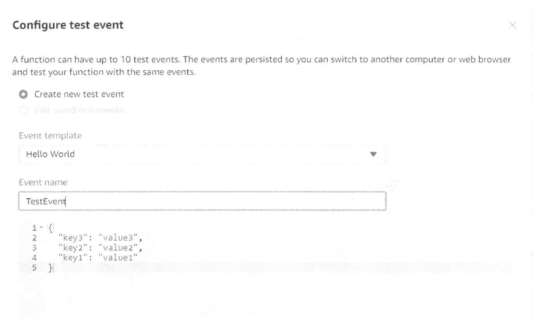

**Figure 2.49: Creating a test event named TestEvent**

8.  Click on the **Test** button now, and you should see the following screen:

**Figure 2.50: The test execution was successful notification**

9. Expand the execution result. Here, you can find more details about the function executions. Here, you can review the duration of the function's execution, the resources that have been configured, billed duration, and max memory used:

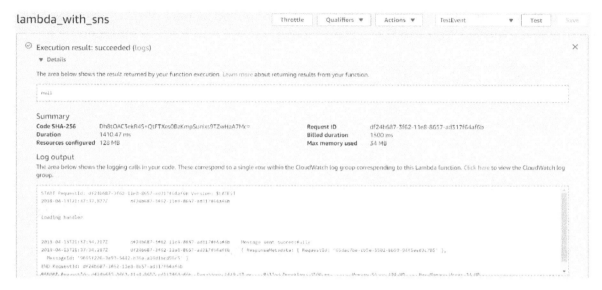

Figure 2.51: Summary of test execution

10. Review the execution results under the **Function code** section as well:

Figure 2.52: Reviewing the test execution results under the function code

As we can see, the following message in the execution results is **Message sent successfully**. This confirms that the Lambda code was successful in sending a notification to the SNS topic.

Time to check your email account, which was configured as part of the subscriber in the preview exercise. You should see the following AWS notification message:

Figure 2.53: Sample email from the SNS service named TestSNS

This concludes our exercise on the simple integration of Lambda with Amazon SNS.

## Activity 3: Setting Up a Mechanism to Get an Email Alert When an Object Is Uploaded into an S3 Bucket

In the last exercise, we showcased lambda integration with Amazon SNS. As part of the exercise, whenever our lambda function was executed, we got an email alert generated by SNS service.

Now, we will extend that exercise to perform an activity here.

Let's assume that you are processing certain events and whenever there is an error with processing of a particular event, you move the problematic event into a S3 bucket so you can process them separately. Also, you want to be notified via an email whenever any such an event arrives in the S3 bucket.

So, we will do an activity to create a new S3 bucket and set up a mechanism that enables you to get an email alert whenever a new object is uploaded into this S3 bucket. When a new object is added to the S3 bucket, it will trigger the Lambda function created in the earlier exercise which will send the required email alert using SNS service.

Here are the steps for completion:

1.  Go to AWS S3 service and click on **Create bucket**.

2.  Provide details such as name and region.

3.  Select the appropriate permissions.

4.  Go to the Lambda function created in the earlier exercise. Add S3 as a trigger under Lambda configuration section.

5.  Add the required details related to S3 bucket configuration, mainly the bucket name.

6.  Click on Add to add that S3 bucket as a trigger to execute Lambda function.

7.  Click on **Save** to save the changes to the Lambda function.

8.  Now, try to upload a new sample file to the S3 bucket. You should see an email alert in your mailbox.

> **Note**
>
> The solution for this activity can be found on page 154.

## Summary

In this chapter, we looked at Amazon S3 and serverless deployments. We worked with API Gateway and its integration with AWS. We delved into fully managed services such as SNS, SQS, and DynamoDB. Finally, we integrated SNS with S3 and Lambda.

In the next chapter, we'll build an API Gateway that we covered in this chapter. A comparison with a traditional on-premises web application will be done as we replace traditional servers with serverless tools while making the application scalable, highly available, and performant.

# 3

# Building and Deploying a Media Application

**Learning Objectives**

By the end of this chapter, you will be able to:

- Explain the challenges of a traditional web application and making a traditional application serverless
- Build an API Gateway API and upload binary data using it
- Work with media processing using AWS Lambda
- Explain image processing using AWS Rekognition

This chapter teaches you how to deploy your first serverless project step by step, by building a simple serverless application that uploads and processes media files.

## Introduction

Enterprises can face tremendous pressure and challenges when building and scaling even simple media-based applications. The conventional ways of building applications require enterprises to invest a lot of time and money up front, so that even simple application development can become a big project for companies.

When it comes to building media-processing applications, which are generally very resource intensive, the situation gets even worse.

In this chapter, we are going to look at the challenges around building such applications and how cloud native development has changed the way applications are built and delivered to customers.

## Designing a Media Web Application – from Traditional to Serverless

Building media web applications in the traditional way follows a certain path. This is displayed in the following diagram:

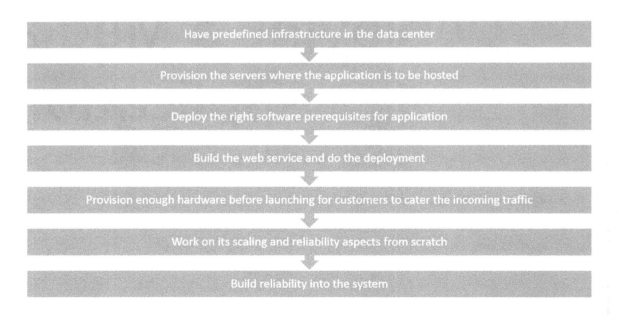

Figure 3.1: Traditional way of building media applications

However, in serverless application development, you don't manage the infrastructure but depend upon cloud providers for it. You have to develop your application to be independently deployable as microservices. During serverless development, you might want to break your big monolithic application into smaller independent business units.

Such a serverless development brings many important patterns as well as development methodologies to be considered. Also, cloud providers provide many managed services at every stage of the software development life cycle to help you build faster with out-of-the-box monitoring/visibility in your serverless infrastructure.

In the next section of this chapter, we will take a look at the steps we need to follow if a media application has to be built in serverless mode. You will see we don't really need to talk to our IT department to raise any infrastructure requests and wait on them for weeks or months. Infrastructure is available with you within minutes from cloud providers.

## Building a Simple Serverless Media Web Application

You have realized by now that by using traditional structures, there is a lot of time-consuming technical administration.

In the cloud era, this is not the case. Cloud providers take care of all the infrastructure, as well as scaling and reliability, and the other needs of your application, so you can focus on the business logic. This not only helps you focus on the right things, but also helps you reduce your time to market drastically.

To depict this, let's do a quick demo of our use case and look at how we can implement it in the AWS Cloud.

We'll deploy our web application locally. Clients will use this application to upload images to AWS. (Figure 3.2 depicts what we want to achieve in this tutorial.) Clients will call the APIs to upload images. These APIs will be hosted in an API Gateway and expose endpoints to upload images to S3. Once the image is uploaded to S3, an event will be triggered by S3 automatically that will launch a Lambda function. This Lambda function will read the image and process it using the AWS Rekognition service to find data inside the image. All the infrastructure required for this is managed by AWS automatically.

Auto scaling and reliability come out of the box by deploying the application on AWS Cloud's global infrastructure:

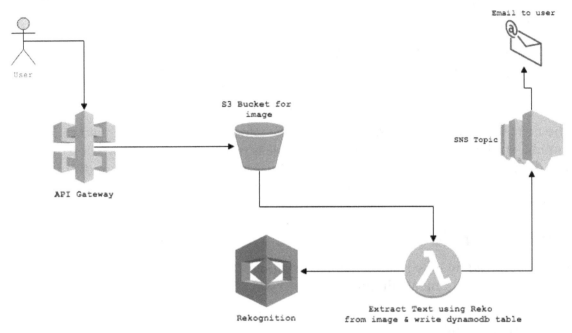

Figure 3.2: Demonstrating working mechanism of serverless media web application

### Exercise 7: Building the Role to Use with an API

In the following demo, we are using the AWS web console to build the role and assign it to the API.

Before you start creating the API, you need to create a proper role to assign to the API when it is created. This role should have access to create/read/update/delete S3 buckets and **APIGatewayInvokeFullAccess**. This role should also have **apigateway. amazonaws.com** added to its trusted entities so that API Gateway can acquire this role.

Here are the steps to perform this exercise:

1. Search for **IAM** in the AWS console and open the **Identity and Access Management** window.

2. Click on **Roles** to view existing roles.

3. Click on **Create role** and select **AWS service** under **Select type of trusted entity**.

4. Select **API Gateway** and click on **Next: Permissions**:

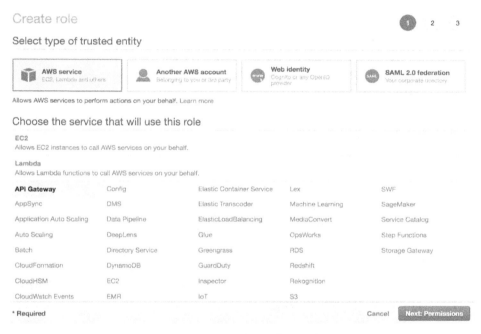

Figure 3.3: Creating role window

5. Click on **Next: Review** without changing anything.

6. Name the role and give a description, as shown in the following screenshot. Name it **api-s3-invoke-demo**:

Figure 3.4: Providing the role information in the Review section

Your role is created. Let's add the required policy to it to work with S3.

7. Click on the newly created role to go to its **Summary** page. On the **Summary** page of that role, click on **Attach Policy**:

Figure 3.5: Summary page of newly created page

8. On the policies page, search and add two policies: **AmazonS3FullAccess** and **AmazonAPIGatewayInvokeFullAccess**.

9. After attaching the policies, the final role summary should be as follows:

Figure 3.6: Summary page view with newly attached policies

## Exercise 8: Creating an API to Push to / Get from an S3 Bucket

In this exercise, we will create an API that will interact with the AWS S3 service.

We will push files to S3 and also create the **GET** method in the API to fetch the contents of the S3 bucket. All this will be serverless, meaning we are not going to provision any EC2 instances, but use AWS's managed serverless infrastructure.

Here are the steps to perform this exercise:

1.  In the **Amazon API Gateway** section of the AWS console, click on the **Create API** button:

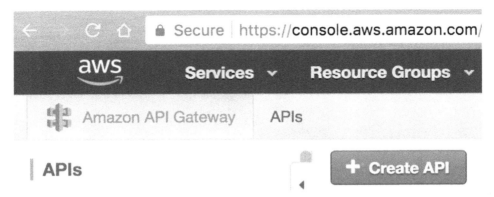

Figure 3.7: Creating a new API from the APIs section

2.  Select the **New AP**I radio and add the following details:

    **API Name**: image-demo

    **Description**: this is a demo api for images

    **Endpoint Type**: **Regional**

Figure 3.8: Creating a new API with specified details

3. Click on **Actions** and select **Create Resource** to create a child resource named **image** and set it as a path variable under the resource path:

Figure 3.9: Creating resource for newly created API

Make sure you add { } in **Resource Path**.

4. Create another child resource of **image** child and name it `file`:

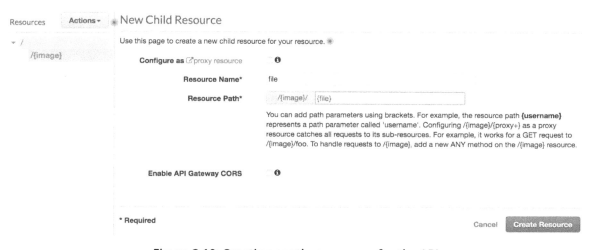

Figure 3.10: Creating another resource for the API

5.  Now that the resource has been created, you need to create methods for your API. Click on **"/{image}"** and from **Actions**, select **Create Method**:

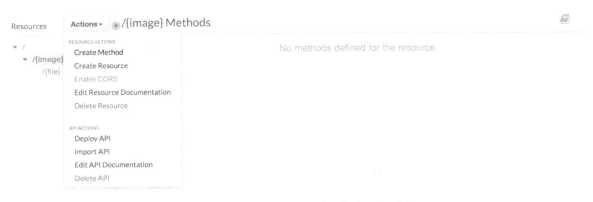

Figure 3.11: Creating methods for the API

6.  Then, select **GET** in the setup and click on the tick mark:

Figure 3.12: Selecting the GET method from the dropdown list

7. Select the integration type as **AWS Service** and fill in the details for the GET method, as shown next. Also, select **Use patch override** under the **Action** type, and fill in the details as **{bucket}** in the execution role. Mention the ARN of the role that was created. Then, click on **Save**:

**Figure 3.13: Selecting options to set up the GET method**

8. Click on **Save**. You should see what is shown in the following screenshot for the GET method:

**Figure 3.14: The Method Execution window of the GET method**

You can see four sections in the preceding screenshot:

**Method Request**

**Integration Request**

**Integration Response**

**Method Response**

9. Go back to **Method Execution** and click on **Method Request**, then add the Content-Type to the **HTTP Request Headers** section:

▼ HTTP Request Headers

| Name | Required | Caching | |
|------|----------|---------|---|
| Content-Type | | | ▤ ✪ |

⊕ **Add header**

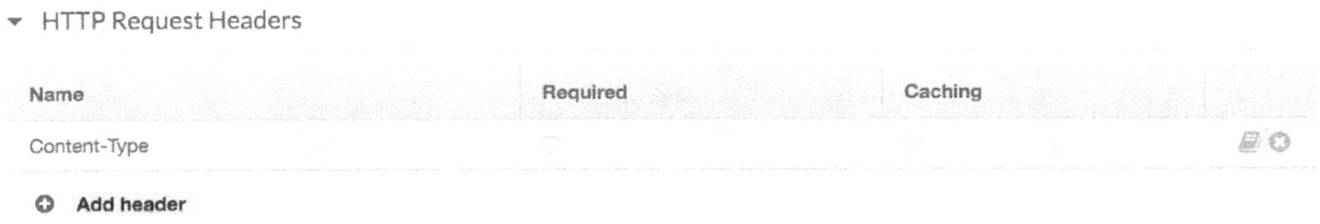

Figure 3.15: HTTP Request Headers section

Now, you need to map the path variable in the **Method Request** to the **Integration Request**. This is required because we want to send the data coming in to the API request to the backend system. **Method Request** represents the incoming data request and **Integration Request** represents the underlying request that is sent to the system actually doing the work. In this case, that system is S3.

10. Click on **Integration Request** and scroll to **URL Path Parameters**. Click on **Add Path** to add following.

**Name**: bucket

**Mapped from**: `method.request.path.image`

11. In **Integration Request** in the **HTTP headers** section, add two headers:

```
x-amz-acl = 'authenticated-read'
Content-Type = method.request.header.Content-Type
```

**Note**

**x-amz-acl** is required to tell S3 that this is the authenticated request. The user needs to be provided read access to the bucket.

Your URL path parameters and HTTP headers for the Integration Request should look as follows now:

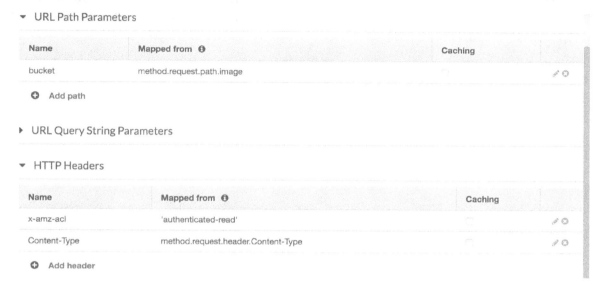

Figure 3.16: HTTP Headers and URL Path Parameters section

12. Repeat steps 5 to 11 to create the **PUT** method. Instead of selecting **GET** in step 6, you have to select **PUT**. We will use this method to create a new bucket.

    Your API should now look like this:

Figure 3.17: Method Execution window of the PUT method

13. Next, create the API to upload the image into the specified bucket. Click on **/ {file}** and then select **Create Method** from the **Action** dropdown. Select the **PUT** method and configure it as shown in the following screenshot. Make note of the path override. It should be set to **{bucket}/{object}**. Role ARN should be same as in previous steps. Click on **Save**.

Figure 3.18: The Setup window of the PUT method

14. In the **Method Request**, add the **HTTP Header** Content-type.

15. Click on **Integration Request**, and add in **URL Path Parameters**, the mapping of the bucket and object as shown here, and click on the tick mark:

```
bucket = method.request.path.image
object = method.request.path.file
```

16. Also, add the **Content-Type** header mapping to `method.request.header.Content-Type` as done earlier for other methods.

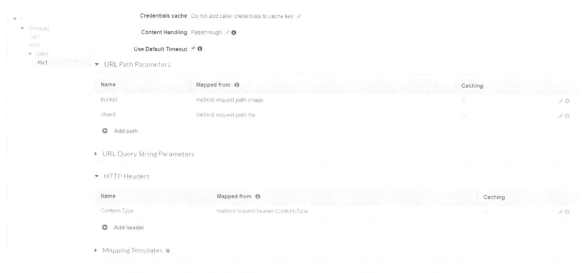

Figure 3.19: Method Request window of the PUT method

One more thing we need to do is to configure the API to accept binary image content.

17. Now, go to **Settings** from the left navigation panel to configure the API to accept binary image content:

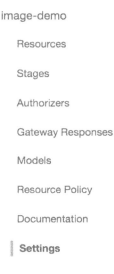

Figure 3.20: Settings options to accept binary image content

18. Add **`image/png`** under **Binary Media Types** and click on **Save Changes**:

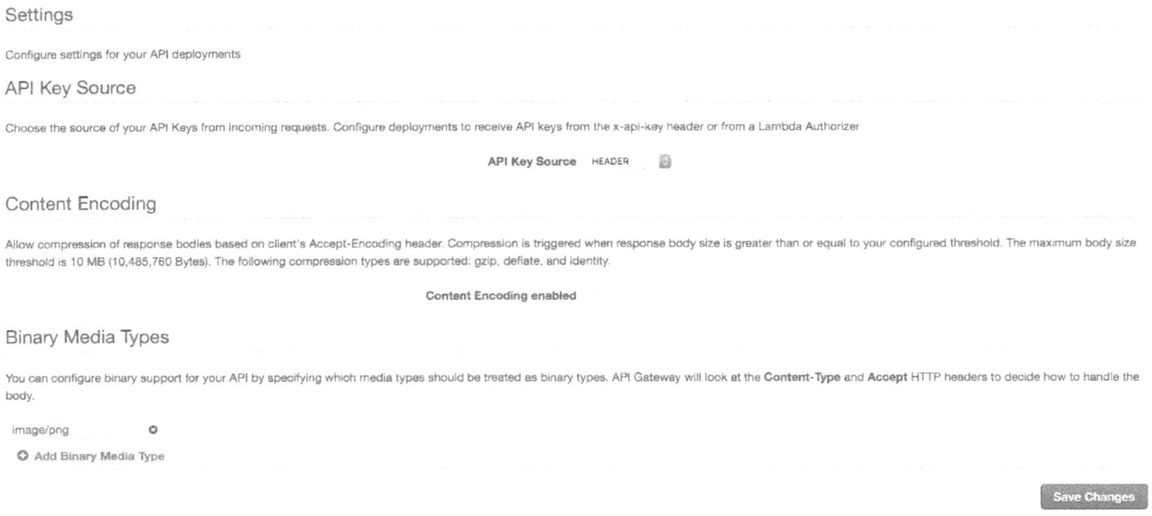

Settings
Configure settings for your API deployments
API Key Source
Choose the source of your API Keys from incoming requests. Configure deployments to receive API keys from the x-api-key header or from a Lambda Authorizer
API Key Source HEADER
Content Encoding
Allow compression of response bodies based on client's Accept-Encoding header. Compression is triggered when response body size is greater than or equal to your configured threshold. The maximum body size threshold is 10 MB (10,485,760 Bytes). The following compression types are supported: gzip, deflate, and identity.
Content Encoding enabled
Binary Media Types
You can configure binary support for your API by specifying which media types should be treated as binary types. API Gateway will look at the Content-Type and Accept HTTP headers to decide how to handle the body.
image/png
Add Binary Media Type
Save Changes

**Figure 3.21: Add the Binary Media Type option under the Binary Media Types section**

All changes are done. We are now ready to deploy our API.

19. Click on **Deploy API** from the **Actions** dropdown:

Resources
Actions
/ Methods
/
/{image}
GET
PUT
/{file}
PUT
RESOURCE ACTIONS
Create Method
Create Resource
Enable CORS
Edit Resource Documentation
API ACTIONS
Deploy API
Import API
Edit API Documentation
Delete API

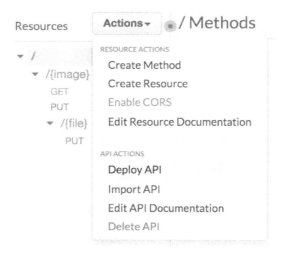

**Figure 3.22: Deploying the API by clicking on the Deploy API option from the Actions dropdown list**

20. Enter the stage details and description, and click on **Deploy**:

Deploy API ⊙

Choose a stage where your API will be deployed. For example, a test version of your API could be deployed to a stage named beta.

| Deployment stage | [New Stage] ⇕ |
|---|---|
| Stage name* | dev |
| Stage description | this is first development stage |
| Deployment description | this is the deployment description |

Cancel **Deploy**

Figure 3.23: Deploying the API after providing all the details

All changes are done. We are now ready to deploy our API.

21. Your API is deployed on the dev stage. Note the Invoke URL:

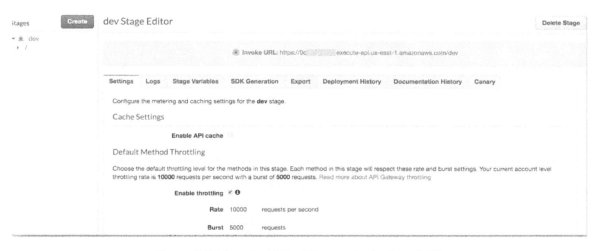

Figure 3.24: Invoke URL of the newly deployed API

22. You can use any API client, such as SoapUI or Postman, for testing your API. We'll use the ReadyAPI tool as it has robust support.

> **Note**
>
> You can download a 14-day free trial at this link: https://smartbear.com/product/ready-api/free-trial/ (you have to enter details of yourself for the download to start).

23. Now, create a bucket. In SoapUI, create a new project for a **PUT** request and enter the invoke URL copied earlier. Enter the bucket name in the path after **/ dev**:

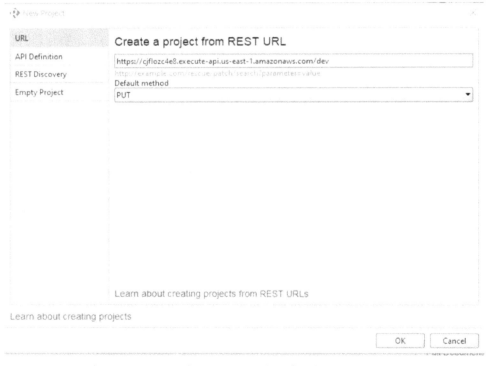

**Figure 3.25: Creating a new project for the PUT request**

24. Click on **OK**. Click on **Continue** to describe your API:

Figure 3.26: Selecting appropriate options for the project

25. Specify the bucket name after **dev/** in **Resource**. In the following screenshot, **mohit-1128-2099** is the bucket name. Change the **Media Type** to **application/xml**:

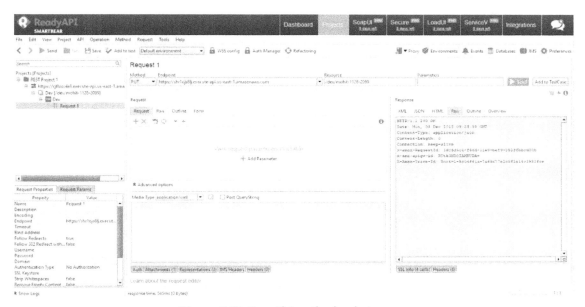

Figure 3.27: Specifying the bucket name

In our exercise, we are creating the S3 bucket in us-east-1. So, we will keep request body as blank. However, if you want to create the bucket in some other region (us-west-, 1 in our, example below), you have to set following text in the request body and hit send. You should get **HTTP 200 Response** status and your bucket should be created in S3:

```
<CreateBucketConfiguration>
<LocationConstraint>us-west-1</LocationConstraint>
</CreateBucketConfiguration>
```

Now the S3 bucket should get created. Go to the AWS S3 service and check the existence of the bucket. You can also do a GET API call to check the existence of the bucket along with its contents.

26. Now, make another call to our API to upload an image. Update the path in the **Resource** textbox of **ReadyAPI** to include the filename that you want to upload in the S3 bucket. You need to attach the file and set the media-type to **image/png**. Go to the **Attachments** tab at the bottom of the request, and attach any PNG image. Click **No** on the **Cache request** dialog box.

27. Click on **Send** and you should be able to get back **200 OK** response. Go back to the AWS S3 service and you should see the newly created bucket now:

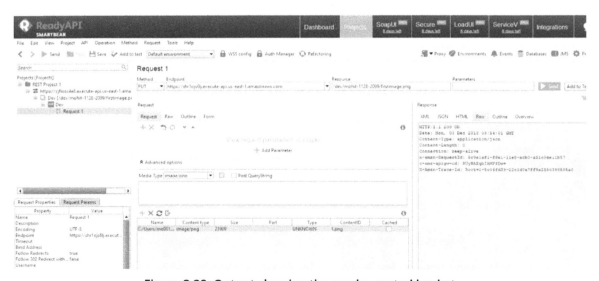

Figure 3.28: Output showing the newly created bucket

So far, we have created an API with the **GET** and **PUT** methods that is accepting requests from the user and uploading images to S3. Note that we haven't had to spawn a server so far for building the entire working service.

## Exercise 9: Building the Image Processing System

You have just created the API. Now, you need to create the backend Lambda function that gets triggered every time an image is uploaded.

This function will be responsible for analyzing the image and detecting the labels inside the image, such as objects. It will call the Rekognition API and feed the image into it, which will then analyze the image and return data.

The returned data will be pushed to a topic in SNS. SNS is AWS Simple Notification Service and works on the pub/sub mechanism. We will then subscribe our email address to that SNS so any messages that are sent to the topic get delivered to our email address also.

The final functionality will be that when a user uploads an image using the API to the S3 bucket, our infrastructure analyzes it and emails us the data found in the image.

We are going to create this infrastructure step by step, as follows:

1. Create the IAM role. As we created the role for API Gateway, we need to follow similar steps; however, we have to select Lambda on the first screen under **Choose the service that will use this role**, and the permissions should be `AWSLambdaFullAccess`, `AmazonRekognitionFullAccess`, and `AmazonSNSFullAccess`. No need to add any tags for now. This is how your role should look after creation:

Figure 3.29: Summary of the newly created ARN role

2. Use the S3 bucket created with our API.

   One more thing before creating the Lambda function is to create an SNS and subscribe your email to it. This SNS will be used by the Lambda to publish image analysis data. Once published, the SNS will send that message to your subscribed email.

3. Go to the SNS console and click on **Create Topic** to publish the extracted text:

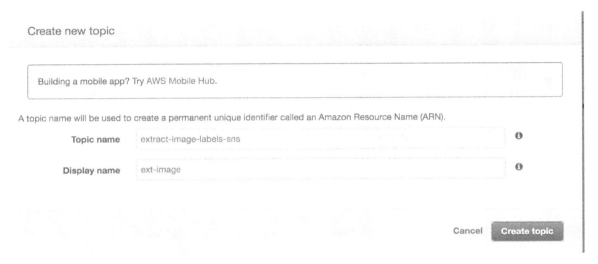

**Figure 3.30: Create new topic window**

4. Click on **Create subscription**:

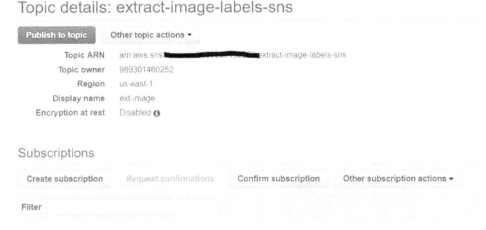

**Figure 3.31: Topic details window**

5.  Create the subscription for the topic. Choose **Email** under **Protocol** and provide an email address under **Endpoint**. There will be an email sent your email account. You have to confirm the subscription:

Create subscription

| Topic ARN | arn:aws:sns:us-east-1: :extract-image-labels-sns |
| Protocol | Email ▼ |
| Endpoint | ....m |

Cancel  **Create subscription**

**Figure 3.32: Create subscription window**

6.  Keep a note of the Topic ARN as it will be required in the Lambda code.

    We have created an API Gateway API, S3 bucket, SNS Topic, and email subscription. Now, we have to create a Lambda function.

7.  In the Lambda console, click on **Create function**. Make sure that you have the same region selected as the one in which you have created the S3 bucket. Select **Author from scratch**.

8. In the next wizard, fill the name of the Lambda, choose an existing role, and choose the S3 bucket name that you created:

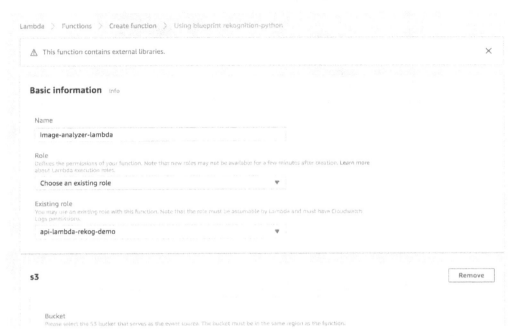

Figure 3.33: Screenshot of the Using blueprint rekognition-python window

9. Scroll to the end and hit **Create function**.

10. In the configuration section of the Lambda, go to the function code and replace it with the following code. In the code, we create the SDK object, AWS Rekognition client, and AWS SNS client. We then handle the incoming Lambda request. We create the bucket and image names. We call the **detectLabels** function to get all the labels using the AWS Rekognition service. Create the message to post and publish to the SNS. The **detectLabels** function is used to make the call to the Rekognition service using the bucket name:

```
var A = require('aws-sdk');
var rek = new A.Rekognition();
var sns = new A.SNS();
AWS.config.update({region: 'us-east-1'});
```

```javascript
exports.handler = (event, context, callback) => {
    console.log('Hello, this is nodejs!');
    // Get the object from the event
    var bucket = event['Records'][0]['s3']['bucket']['name'];
    var imageName = event['Records'][0]['s3']['object']['key'];
    detectLabels(bucket, imageName)
        .then(function(response){
            var params = {
      Message: JSON.stringify(response['Labels']), /* required */
      Subject: imageName,
      TopicArn: 'arn:aws:sns:us-east-1:XXXXXXXXXXXX:extract-image-labels-
sns'
};

    sns.publish(params, function(err, data) {
  if (err) console.log(err, err.stack); // an error occurred
  else      console.log(data);           // successful response
});
        });

    callback(null, 'Hello from Lambda');
};


function detectLabels(bucket, key) {
  let params = {
    Image: {
      S3Object: {
        Bucket: bucket,
        Name: key
      }
    }
  };

  return rekognition.detectLabels(params).promise();
}
```

11. Another thing to note is in the Lambda configuration in the **S3** section. Make sure the trigger is enabled. If it is not, toggle the button to enable it:

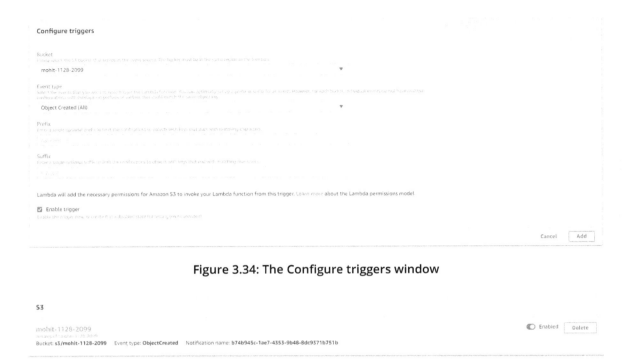

**Figure 3.34: The Configure triggers window**

**Figure 3.35: Enabling the S3 trigger for the Lambda function**

> **Note**
>
> Make sure the S3 bucket is in the same region as the Lambda, or it won't be able to trigger the Lambda.

This concludes the creation of all the infrastructure.

Now, when you call the API to upload any image, you should see an email in your inbox with content similar to this:

**Figure 3.36: Sample email after uploading an image**

## Deployment Options in the Serverless Architecture

We have seen how we can create a serverless application using the AWS console. This is not the only way to achieve it. In the cloud world, infrastructure automation is a key aspect of any deployment. Cloud providers have built strong frameworks around their services that can be used to script out the entire infrastructure. AWS provides APIs, SDKs, and a CLI that can be consumed in various ways to provision infrastructure automatically.

In general, there are three additional ways we can achieve the previous functionality without using the AWS console:

- **AWS CLI**: AWS provides a command-line interface for working with AWS services. It is built on top of an AWS Python SDK called boto. You just need to install Python on your Mac, Windows, or Linux machine and then install the AWS CLI.

  Once installed, you can run the following command in your Terminal or command line to check it is properly installed:

  ```
  $ aws --version
  aws-cli/1.11.96 Python/2.7.10 Darwin/16.7.0 botocore/1.8.2
  ```

- **AWS Code SDKs**: AWS provides many SDKs that can be used directly in your favorite programing language for working with AWS services. As of today, these are the programing languages AWS supports:

  .NET

  Java

  C++

  JavaScript

Python

Ruby

Go

Node.js

PHP

- **Serverless Framework**: This is one option that is becoming more popular by the day. It is a command-line tool that can be used to build and deploy serverless cloud services. It can be used not only with AWS, but also with many other major cloud providers, such as Azure, **Google Cloud Platform** (**GCP**), and IBM Cloud.

It is built in JavaScript and requires Node.js v6.5.0 or later to be installed. For deployment, you provide a YAML-based file, `serverless.yml`, to the CLI. It internally translates all the content of YAML into an AWS CloudFormation template and uses it to provision the infrastructure.

It is again a very powerful tool for working with serverless AWS-managed services.

Like the AWS CLI, it can also be very nicely integrated into a CI/CD process in an enterprise to achieve automation.

## Activity 4: Creating an API to Delete the S3 Bucket

Create an API to delete the S3 bucket that we just created in the preceding exercise. In this activity, you need to expose an API that will accept the bucket name and will delete the S3 bucket.

Here are the steps to complete the activity:

1. Go to the AWS API Gateway console and in the API created in this chapter, create a Delete API.
2. Configure the incoming headers and path parameters properly in the **Method Request** and **Integration Request** sections.
3. Change the authorization of the `Delete` method from `NONE` to `AWS_IAM`.
4. Click on the Deploy API.
5. Test the `Delete` method using the Test Tool (Ready API).

You should see the bucket getting deleted in the AWS S3 console.

> **Note**
>
> The solution for this activity can be found on page 157.

## Summary

In this chapter, you have seen the challenges of traditional web application development and how serverless development can address them. You also learned how to work with API Gateway and expose a REST-based API with it. You integrated AWS S3 with API Gateway and created and read a bucket using **PUT** and **GET** APIs.
We then created Lambda functions. We worked with AWS Rekognition in the event-based architecture to analyze images at runtime and identify important data inside them.

In the next chapter, we'll explore the capabilities of AWS Athena. We'll also work with AWS Glue, and learn how to populate the AWS Glue Data Catalog.

# Serverless Amazon Athena and the AWS Glue Data Catalog

**Learning Objectives**

By the end of this chapter, you will be able to:

- Explain serverless AWS Athena capabilities, as well as its storage and querying concepts
- Access Amazon Athena and its different use cases
- Create databases and tables in Athena
- Explain AWS Glue and its benefits
- Work with data catalogs and populate the AWS Glue Data Catalog

This chapter delves into the capabilities of AWS Athena. You'll also work with AWS Glue, and learn how to populate the AWS Glue Data Catalog.

## Introduction

Consider a situation where you're just about to leave for the day from the office, and at that very moment your boss asks you to run a report on a new, complex dataset. You're asked to finish this report before you leave for the day.

In the past, completing such a report would've taken hours. You would have to first analyze the data, create a schema, and then dump the data before you could execute queries to create the required report.

Now, with the AWS Glue and Athena services, you can get such reports done very quickly and leave for the day on time.

In the previous chapter, we saw how serverless application development can address the challenges of traditional application development. In this chapter, we'll explore the capabilities of AWS Athena. We'll also work with AWS Glue, and learn how to populate the AWS Glue Data Catalog.

## Amazon Athena

In simple terms, Amazon Athena is nothing but an interactive query service that is serverless. It makes use of standard SQL to analyze data in Amazon S3. It allows you to quickly query structured, unstructured, and semi-structured data that is stored in S3. With Athena, you don't need to load any datasets locally or write any complex **ETLs** (**Extracts, Transforms, and Loads**) as it provides the capability to read data directly from S3.

> **Note**
>
> ETL is a popular concept from the data warehouse world, where three separate functions are used to prepare data for data analysis. The term extract refers to data extraction from the source dataset, transform refers to data transformation (if required), and load refers to data loading in the final tables, which will be used for data analysis.

The Amazon Athena service uses Presto technology. Presto is a distributed SQL query engine that is open source. Presto provides a SQL-like dialect for querying data and is designed to provide fast performance for running interactive analytic queries. The size of the data sources doesn't matter. The AWS management console, Athena API, Athena CLI, or a simple JDBC connection can be used to access Amazon Athena.

Athena is a serverless offering, meaning that you don't need to set up or manage any underlying data servers. What you must do is set up a connection to your data in Amazon S3. Then, you must define the schema. Once you've done that, you can start querying with the help of the query editor in the AWS management console. You can use ANSI SQL queries with Amazon Athena, including the support of joins and functions, to query data in S3. Therefore, it's easy for anyone with basic skills in SQL to analyze large-scale datasets quickly.

Amazon Athena supports multiple data formats such as CSV, JSON, and Parquet. With Athena, you can query encrypted data (be it encrypted on the server side or client side). Amazon Athena also gives you the option to encrypt your result sets by integrating with **KMS** (**Key Management Service**):

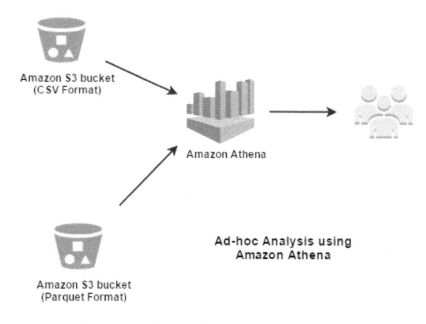

Figure 4.1: Ad hoc analysis using Amazon Athena

> **Note**
>
> Amazon Athena is priced per query. You will be charged for the data scanned per query. As you might've noticed, data can be stored in different formats on Amazon S3. Therefore, you can use different formats to store data in a compressed form, resulting in lower amounts of data being scanned by your query. You can partition your data or convert your data to columnar storage formats to read only the columns that are required to process the data. Amazon Athena costs start from $5/TB of data scanned.

AWS provides native integration of Athena with the AWS Glue Data Catalog. The AWS Glue Data Catalog provides you with a metadata store that is persistent for your data in Amazon S3. You can, thereby, create tables and query data in Athena. We will study this concept in more detail later in this chapter, along with an exercise.

Here are some of the use cases of Amazon Athena:

- Ad hoc analysis

- Analyzing server logs

- Understanding unstructured data – works well with complex data types such as arrays or maps

- Quick reporting

Here are some of the tools that are used to access Amazon Athena:

- AWS Management Console

- A JDBC or ODBC connection

- API

- Command-line interface

## Databases and Tables

Amazon Athena allows you to create databases and tables. A database is basically a grouping of tables. By default, we have a **sampledb** database that has been created in Athena, but you can create a new database and start creating your tables underneath it if you like. Also, you will find a table called **elb_logs** under **sampledb**:

Figure 4.2: The Database page

## Exercise 10: Creating a New Database and Table Using Amazon Athena

Let's go ahead and create a new database and table so that we can understand Athena, alongside a quick demo, in more detail. Athena works on data that's stored in S3. Before going to Athena, let's create an S3 bucket and upload the sample dataset that's provided. In this exercise, we will use the `flavors_of_cacao.csv` dataset that was provided with this book:

1.  Go to AWS services and search for `Athena`.

    You should be able to see the following window:

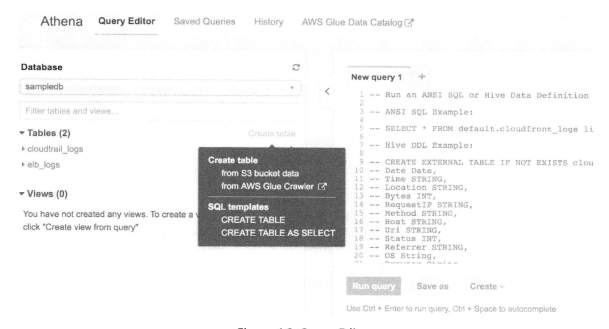

Figure 4.3: Query Editor

2.  Now, click on **Create table** and choose **Manually**.

    > **Note**
    >
    > We will look into the `Automatically (AWS Glue crawler)` option in the next part of this chapter.

3.  Provide the required details, such as the database name, table name, and S3 bucket details. You need to provide the S3 bucket's details in the same place where you have the data stored that you want to analyze via Athena.

4.  Click on the **Next** button.

    You can create the table under the default (already selected) database as well:

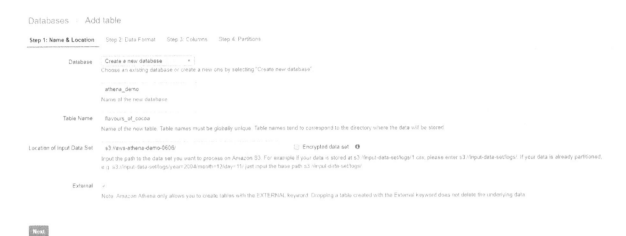

**Figure 4.4: Add table**

> **Note**
>
> The table name needs to be unique here, so choose a different table name than what you see here. Before creating the table, I uploaded the **flavors_of_cacao. csv** dataset into my S3 bucket, that is, **s3://aws-athena-demo-0606/**. However, you can make any changes in the underlying dataset post table creation, as long as you don't change the underlying schema. We will look at this in more detail.

5.  Click on **Next**, and you will see the different data formats that you can access using AWS Athena.

6. Choose **CSV** and click on **Next**:

**Figure 4.5: Data Format**

7. On the next screen, define the columns, along with their data types. Either you can define all of the columns one by one, or you can click on the **Bulk add columns** option to add all of the columns' details into one place.

We have nine columns in our datasets, so we will add the following information, along with their data types:

```
Company string,Bean_Origin string,REF int,Review_Date int,Cocoa_Percent
string,Company_Location string,Rating decimal,Bean_Type string,Broad_Bean_
Origin string
```

Note that the header is removed from the data file. The column details can be understood from the following screenshot:

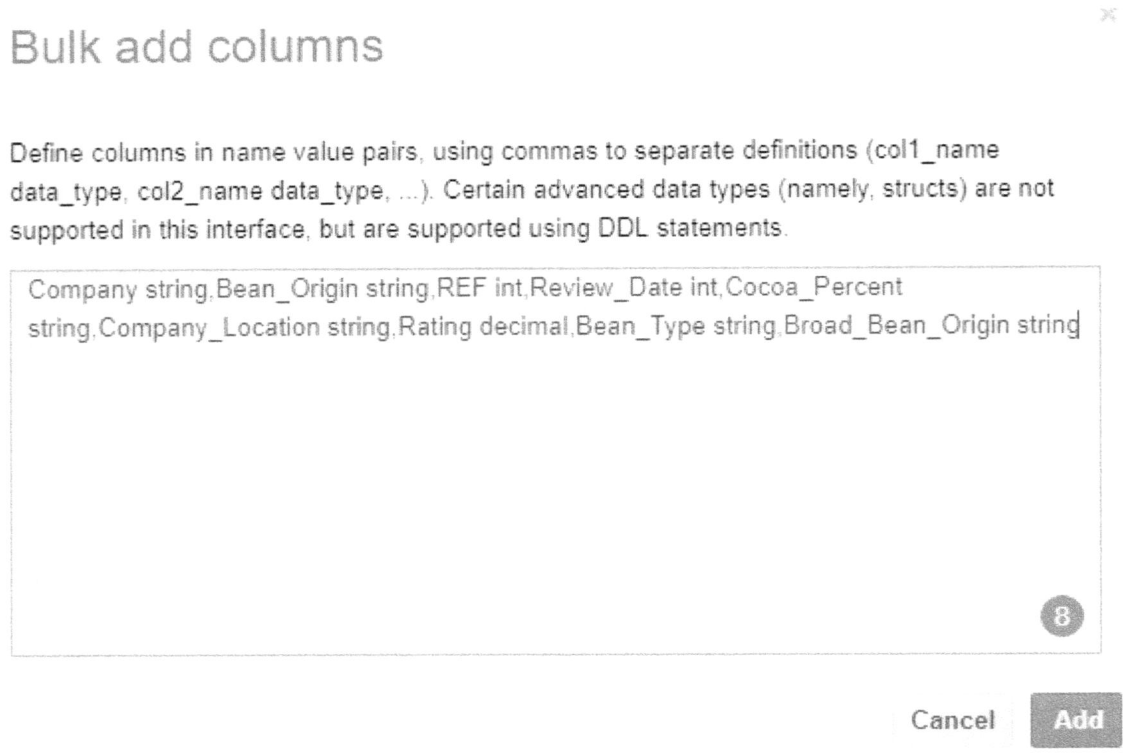

## Bulk add columns

Define columns in name value pairs, using commas to separate definitions (col1_name data_type, col2_name data_type, ...). Certain advanced data types (namely, structs) are not supported in this interface, but are supported using DDL statements.

```
Company string,Bean_Origin string,REF int,Review_Date int,Cocoa_Percent
string,Company_Location string,Rating decimal,Bean_Type string,Broad_Bean_Origin string
```

Cancel    Add

Figure 4.6: Bulk add columns

8. Once you click on the **Add** button, you will note that all of the columns, along with their data types, are displayed. You can make any changes (as required) here as well:

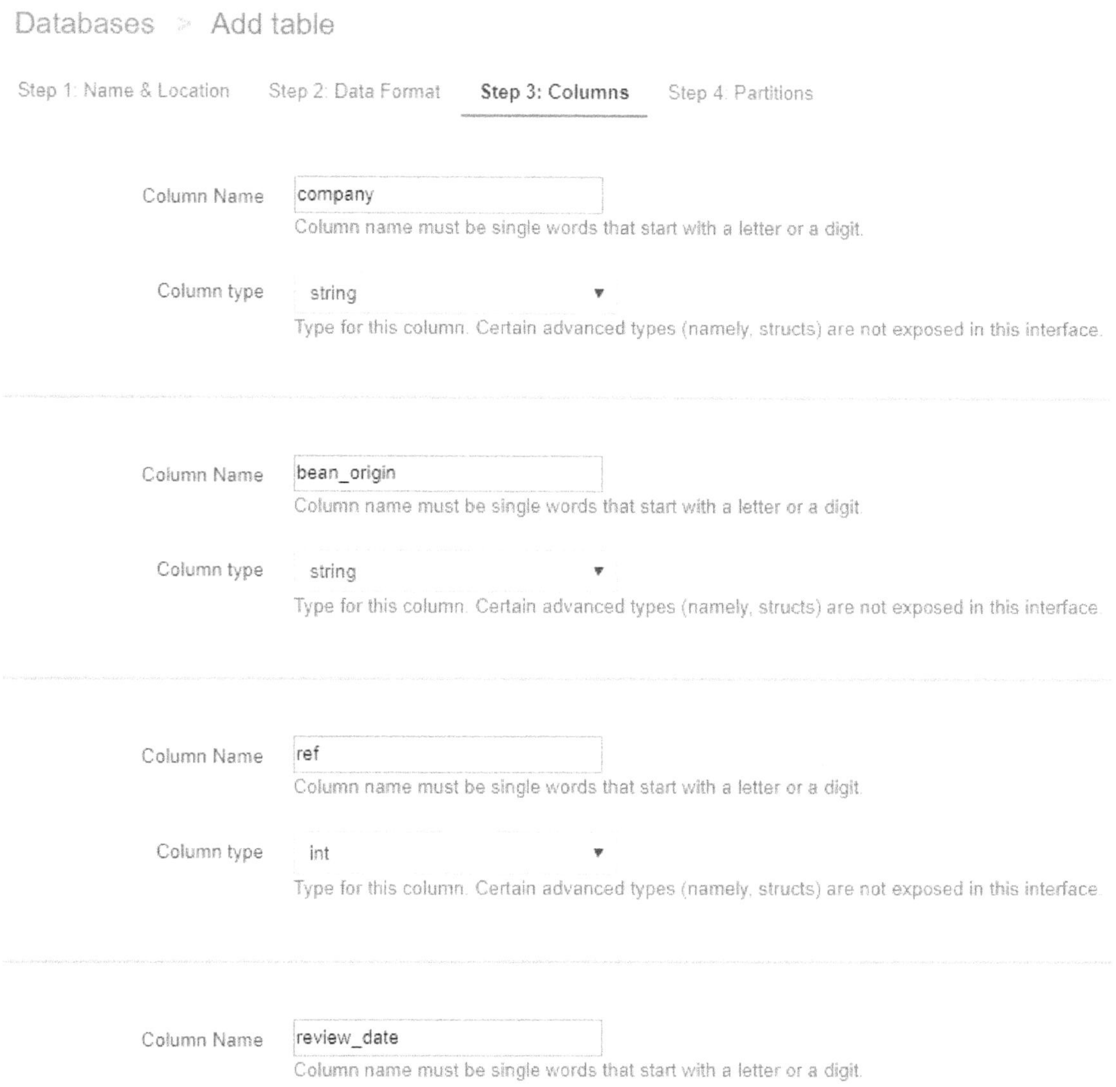

Databases > Add table

Step 1: Name & Location   Step 2: Data Format   **Step 3: Columns**   Step 4: Partitions

Column Name    company

Column name must be single words that start with a letter or a digit.

Column type    string   ▼

Type for this column. Certain advanced types (namely, structs) are not exposed in this interface.

Column Name    bean_origin

Column name must be single words that start with a letter or a digit.

Column type    string   ▼

Type for this column. Certain advanced types (namely, structs) are not exposed in this interface.

Column Name    ref

Column name must be single words that start with a letter or a digit.

Column type    int   ▼

Type for this column. Certain advanced types (namely, structs) are not exposed in this interface.

Column Name    review_date

Column name must be single words that start with a letter or a digit.

Figure 4.7: The Columns section

9. Click on **Next**. You can configure partitions on this screen. Partitions allow you to create logical groups of information together, which helps with the faster retrieval of information. Partitions are generally recommended for larger datasets.

   However, since our dataset is quite small, we will skip configuring partitions for now:

**Figure 4.8: Partitions**

10. Click on **Create Table** and Athena will run the **create table** statement. Your table will be created. Now, you should see following screen:

**Figure 4.9: Run query**

Here, we can note that our database, **Athena_demo**, has been created, and a new table, **flavours_of_cocoa**, has been created as well. You can see the table definition on the right of the screen.

> **Note**
>
> If you don't want to go through GUI for table creation, you can write the table **Data Definition Language** (**DDL**) directly into the query window and create the table. You can also use the **ALTER** and **DROP TABLE** commands to modify and drop the existing tables, respectively.

11. Click on the **Save as** button and provide a name for the query:

**Figure 4.10: Choosing a name window**

Now, the table has been created, and you can run SQL statements to view the table data.

12. In the following screenshot, you will see the 10 rows that have been selected from the table:

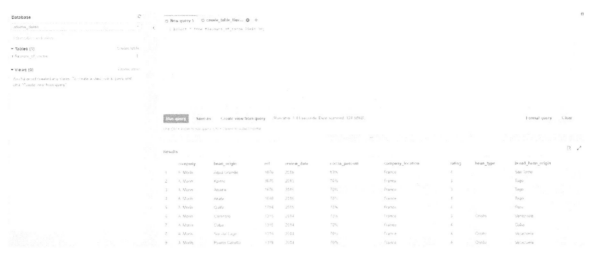

Figure 4.11: Selecting 10 rows

13. Write SQL functions as well to analyze the data from different perspectives. Here, we will list the total products of a company that have a rating greater than 4 by performing a **group by** operation on the company and getting the required count:

```
select company, count(*) cnt from flavours_of_cocoa
where rating > 4
group by company
order by cnt desc
limit 10;
```

14. Execute the query.

You'll see the following output in the result pane:

Figure 4.12: Output window

Since Athena is based on hive SQL and Presto, you can use many of the Hive functions with Athena.

> **Note**
>
> For the complete documentation on supported SQL queries, functions, and operators, go to https://docs.aws.amazon.com/athena/latest/ug/functions-operators-reference-section.html.

With this, we have completed our exercise on AWS Athena. As we stated earlier in this chapter, Athena is a wonderful query service that simplifies analyzing data from Amazon S3 directly.

Be aware that you get charged on the amount of data being analyzed for your query. In the preceding query, you can see the highlighted part for the amount of data being scanned by the query. However, if you don't apply the proper filters, you can end up scanning unnecessarily huge amounts of data, which eventually escalates the overall costs.

# AWS Glue

AWS Glue is a serverless, cloud-optimized, and fully managed ETL service that provides automatic schema inference for your structured and semi-structured datasets. AWS Glue helps you understand your data, suggests transformations, and generates ETL scripts so that you don't need to do any ETL development.

You can also set up AWS Glue for running your ETL jobs, automatically provisioning and scaling the resources needed to complete them. You can point AWS Glue to your data that's stored on different AWS services such as S3, RDS, and Redshift. It finds out what your data is. It stores the related metadata, such as schemas and table definitions, in the AWS Glue Data Catalog.

Once your data is cataloged, you can start using it for different kinds of data analysis. For executing data transformations and data loading processes, AWS Glue generates code.

First, let's understand the major components of AWS Glue, which might be new to the students:

- **AWS Glue Data Catalog**: A data catalog is used to organize your data. Generally, glue crawlers populate data catalogs, but you can use DDL statements as well to populate it. You can bring in metadata information from multiple data sources such as Amazon S3, Redshift, or RDS instances, and create a single data catalog for all of them. Now, all of the metadata is in one place and is searchable. The Glue catalog is basically a replacement for Hive Metastore.

  > **Note**
  >
  > A data catalog is mainly comprised of metadata information (definitions) related to database objects such as tables, views, procedures, indexes, and synonyms. Almost all databases in the market today have data catalogs populated in the form of information schema. Data catalogs help users to understand and consume data for their analysis. It is a very popular concept in the big data world.

- **AWS Glue Crawlers**: Crawlers are primarily used to connect with different data sources, discover the schema, and partition and store associated metadata into the data catalogs. Crawlers detect schema changes and version updates, and keep the data catalog in sync. They also detect if data is partitioned in the underlying tables.

Crawlers have data classifiers written to infer the schemas for several popular data formats such as relational data stores, JSON, and Parquet format. You can also write a custom data classifier for a custom file format (using Grok pattern) that Glue doesn't recognize and associates it with the crawler. You can write multiple classifiers and, once your data is classified, Glue will ignore subsequent data classifiers.

You can run Glue crawlers on an ad hoc basis or on a particular schedule. Moreover, with Glue crawlers being serverless, you only pay when they are in use.

The following diagram depicts the complete workflow for AWS Glue:

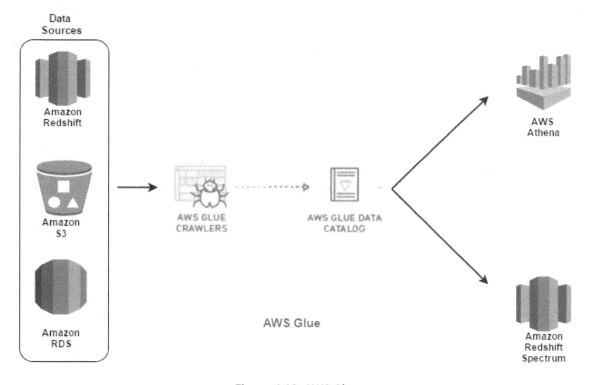

Figure 4.13: AWS Glue

In the preceding diagram, we have multiple data sources such as Amazon S3, Redshift, and RDS instances, which are connected by AWS Glue crawlers to read and populate the AWS Glue data catalogs. Also, you can use Amazon Athena or AWS Redshift Spectrum to access AWS Glue data catalogs for the purpose of data analysis.

## Exercise 11: Using AWS Glue to Build a Metadata Repository

Let's look at an example of how AWS Glue automatically identifies data formats and schemas and then builds a metadata repository, thereby eliminating the need to manually define and maintain schemas. We will use the same **chocolate-barratings** dataset that we used previously for our Glue exercise:

1.  Log in to the AWS Management Console and go to AWS Glue service.

2.  Go to **Crawlers** and click on **Add crawler** to open the **Add crawler** screen. Let's name the crawler **chocolate_ratings**:

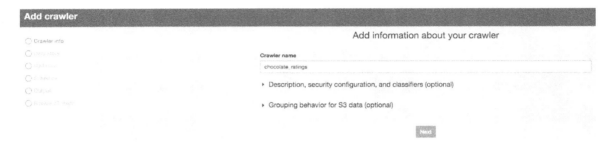

Figure 4.14: Crawler information

3.  Click on **Next**. Here, you can specify the Amazon S3 path where your dataset is located. We can either use the S3 picker (highlighted in yellow) for this or just paste in the S3 path:

Figure 4.15: Adding a data store

4. Click on **Next**. If you have data across multiple S3 buckets or other data sources such as RDS and Redshift, you can add them on this screen. We will only go with a single S3 source for this demonstration for now:

Figure 4.16: Adding another data store

5. On the next screen, define an IAM role for the crawler. This role provides the crawler with the required permissions to access the different data stores. Click on **Next**:

Figure 4.17: Choosing an IAM role

6. Now, set up the schedule for the crawler. We can either run this crawler on demand or on schedule. If we automatically schedule a crawler, it helps us to identify any changes to the underlying data and keeps the data catalog up to date. This automatic update of the data catalog is very helpful for datasets that change on frequently. We will run it on demand for now:

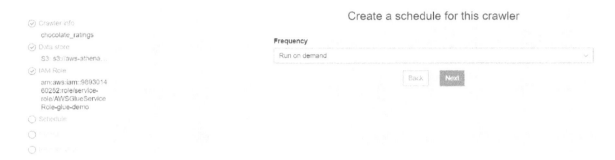

**Figure 4.18: Creating a schedule for the crawler**

7. Here, you can either select an existing database to keep the data catalog or create a new one. We will create a new database called **glue-demo** for this demonstration. Also, if you want to add a prefix to all of the tables that have been created by crawler for easy identification, you can add the prefix here. We will skip this:

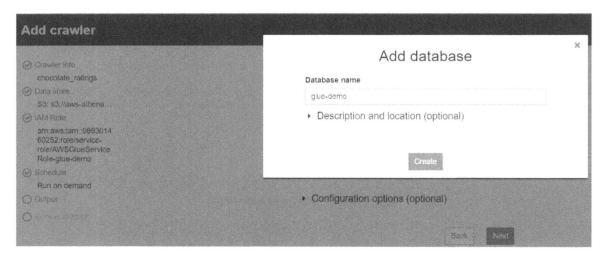

**Figure 4.19: Adding a database**

8. Also, as we discussed earlier in this chapter, crawlers can handle changes to the schemas to ensure that table metadata is always in sync with the underlying data. As you can see in the following screenshot, the default settings allow crawlers to modify the catalogue schemas if the underlying data is updated or deleted. We can disable it as well, based on our needs:

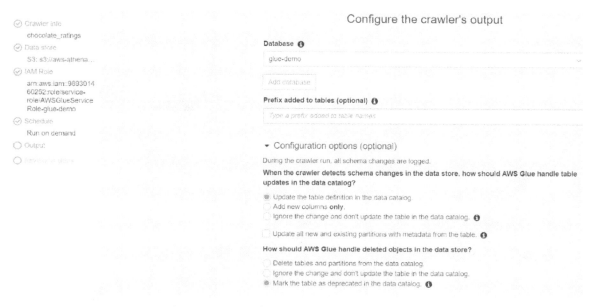

Figure 4.20: Configuring the crawler's output

9. Click on **Next** to review the crawler specifications and click on **Finish** to create the crawler:

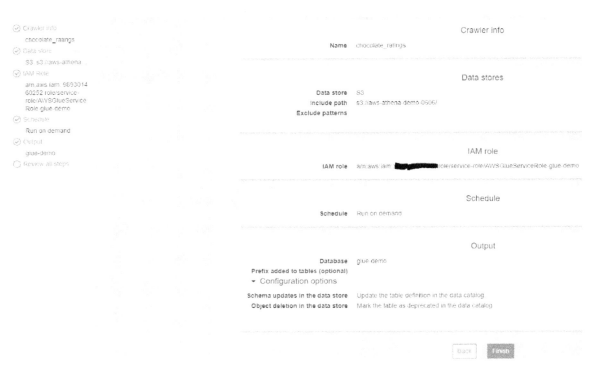

Figure 4.21: Review all of the steps

10. Now that the crawler has been created, let's go ahead and run it. Once the crawler has completed running, you will notice in the following screenshot that one new table has been added in the data catalog. This table is a metadata representation of data and points to the location where the data is physically located:

Figure 4.22: Adding the crawler

11. Go to **Tables** and click the `aws_athena_demo_0606` table to take a look at the schema that has been populated by the crawlers:

Figure 4.23: Editing the table

You can also change the data type of any column as required here. Also, you can view the partitions associated with the table.

Since our table is defined in the catalog, we can query it using Amazon Redshift Spectrum or Amazon Athena. Both products allow you to query data directly from S3. We already looked at how to query it using Amazon Athena earlier in this chapter. The only difference will be that the database name will be different this time. Please go ahead and try it yourself.

Now, we have seen how AWS Glue makes it easy to crawl data and maintain metadata information in the data catalog. Although there are multiple other ways to populate your catalog with tables such as manually defining the table, importing from an external Hive Metastore, or running Hive DDL queries to create the catalog, AWS Glue provides an easy to use method to create and maintain data catalogs on a regular basis. This concludes our discussion on AWS Glue.

## Activity 5: Building an AWS Glue Catalog for a CSV-Formatted Dataset and Analyzing the Data Using AWS Athena

Imagine you are a data analyst. You have been provided with a dataset that contains inventory-to-sales ratios for each month since 1992.

These ratios can be better explained as follows:

*Ratio = Number of months of inventory/Sales for a month*

Considering this, a ratio of 3.5 means that the business has an inventory that will cover three and a half months of sales. You have been asked to quickly review the data. You have to prepare a report to get a count of the months for the last 10 years when the inventories to sales ratio was < **1.25**. For example, if the ratio was low four times in the month of January since 1992, then January 4 should be the result.

A CSV formatted dataset called total business-inventories-to-sales ratio has been provided with this book. This dataset is derived from another dataset that's available on the Kaggle website (https://www.kaggle.com/census/total-business-inventories-and-sales-data). This dataset has two columns:

- **Observed_Data**: Date when the observation was made
- **Observed_Value**: Inventories to sales ratios

Here are the steps to complete this activity:

1. Create an AWS Glue crawler and build a catalog for this dataset. Verify that the data types are reflected correctly.

2. Go to AWS Athena and create a new schema and table for the data, which you cataloged in step 1.

3. Once you have the data exposed in Athena, you can start building your reports.

4. Write a query to filter the data, where the inventories to sales ratios (**observed_values**) was less than 1.25, and group the output by month. Then, you will have the reports ready to share.

> **Note**
>
> The solution for this activity can be found on page 158.

# Summary

In this chapter, we learned about serverless AWS Athena capabilities, its storage, and its querying concepts. We also discussed different use cases for AWS Athena. Later, we learned about AWS Glue and its benefits. We looked at what data catalogs are, their uses, and how to populate the AWS Glue Data Catalog. In the end, we leveraged the catalog that we created via AWS Glue in AWS Athena to access the underlying data and analyze it.

In the next chapter, we'll focus on the capabilities of Amazon Athena and AWS Glue.

# 5

# Real-Time Data Insights Using Amazon Kinesis

**Learning Objectives**

By the end of this chapter, you will be able to:

- Explain the concept of real-time data streams
- Create a Kinesis stream using Amazon Kinesis Data Streams
- Use Amazon Kinesis Data Firehose to create a delivery stream
- Set up an analytics application and process data using Amazon Kinesis Data Analytics

This chapter shows you how to unleash the potential of real-time data insights and analytics using Amazon Kinesis. You'll also combine Amazon Kinesis capabilities with AWS Lambda to create lightweight, serverless architectures.

## Introduction

We live in a world surrounded by data. Whether you are using a mobile app, playing a game, browsing a social networking website, or buying your favorite accessory from an online store, companies have set up different services to collect, store, and analyze high throughput information to stay up to date on customer's choices and behaviors. These types of setups, in general, require complex software and infrastructures that can be expensive to provision and manage.

Many of us have worked on aggregating data from different sources to accomplish reporting requirements, and most of us can attest that this whole data crunching process is often very demanding. However, a more painful trend has been that as soon as the results of this data are found, the information is out of date again. Technology has drastically changed over the last decade, which has resulted in real-time data being a necessity to stay relevant for today's businesses. Moreover, real-time data helps organizations improve on operational efficiency and many other metrics.

We also need to be aware of the diminishing value of data. As time goes on, the value of old data continues to decrease, which makes recent data very valuable; hence, the need for real-time analysis increases even further.

In this chapter, we'll look at how Amazon Kinesis makes it possible to unleash the potential of real-time data insights and analytics, by offering capabilities such as Kinesis Video Streams, Kinesis Data Streams, Kinesis Data Firehose, and Kinesis Data Analytics.

## Amazon Kinesis

Amazon Kinesis is a distributed data streaming platform for collecting and storing data streams from hundreds of thousands of producers. Amazon Kinesis makes it easy to set up high capacity pipes that can be used to collect and analyze your data in real time. You can process incoming feeds at any scale, enabling you to respond to different use cases, such as customer spending alerts and click stream analysis. Amazon Kinesis enables you to provide curated feeds to customers on a real-time basis rather than performing batch processing on large, text-based log files later on. You can just send each event to Kinesis and have it analyzed right away to find patterns and exceptions, and keep an eye on all of your operational details. This will allow you to take decisive action instantly.

## Benefits of Amazon Kinesis

Like other AWS serverless services, Amazon Kinesis has several benefits. Most of the benefits have already been discussed in terms of other services, so I will restrain myself from going into the details. However, here is the list of the benefits of using Amazon Kinesis' services:

- Easy administration

- Low cost

- Security

- Pay as you go capabilities

- Durability

- High scalability

- Choice of framework

- Replayability

- Continuous processing

- Highly concurrent processing

Amazon Kinesis provides different capabilities, depending on different use cases. We will now look at three of the major (and most important) capabilities in detail.

# Amazon Kinesis Data Streams

**Amazon Kinesis Data Streams** is a managed service that makes it easy for you to collect and process real-time streaming data. Kinesis Data Streams enable you to leverage streaming data to power real-time dashboards so that you can look at critical information about your business and make quick decisions. The Kinesis Data Stream can scale easily from megabytes to terabytes per hour, and from thousands to millions of records per second.

You can use Kinesis Data Streams in typical scenarios, such as real-time data streaming and analytics, real-time dashboards, and log analysis, among many other use cases. You can also use Kinesis Data Streams to bring streaming data as input into other AWS services such as **S3**, **Amazon Redshift**, **EMR**, and **AWS Lambda**.

## How Kinesis Data Streams Work

Kinesis Data Streams are made up of one or more **shards**. What is a shard? A shard is a uniquely identified sequence of data records in a stream, providing a fixed unit of capacity. Each shard can ingest data of up to a maximum of 1 MB per second and up to 1,000 records per second, while emitting up to a maximum of 2 MB per second. We can simply increase or decrease the number of shards allocated to your stream in case of changes in input data. The total capacity of the stream is the sum of the capacities of its shards.

By default, Kinesis Data Streams keep your data for up to 24 hours, which enables you to replay this data during that window (in case that's required). You can also increase this retention period to up to 7 days if there is a need to keep the data for longer periods. However, you will incur additional charges for extended windows of data retention.

A **producer** in Kinesis is any application that puts data into the Kinesis Data Streams, and a **consumer** consumes data from the data stream.

The following diagram illustrates the simple functionality of Kinesis Data Streams. Here, we are capturing real-time streaming events from a data source, such as website logs to Amazon Kinesis Streams, and then providing it as input to another AWS Lambda service for interpretation. Then, we are showcasing the results on a **PowerBI dashboard**, or any other dashboard tool:

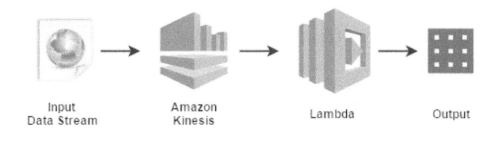

Input
Data Stream

Amazon
Kinesis

Lambda

Output

Amazon Kinesis
Data Streams

**Figure 5.1: An image showing the simple functionality of Kinesis data streams**

## Exercise 12: Creating a Sample Kinesis Stream

Let's go to the AWS console and create a sample Kinesis stream, which will then be integrated with Lambda to move the real-time data into DynamoDB. Whenever an event is published in the Kinesis stream, it will trigger the associated Lambda function, which will then deliver that event to the DynamoDB database.

The following is a high-level diagram showcasing the data flow of our exercise. There are many real-world scenarios that can be accomplished using this architecture:

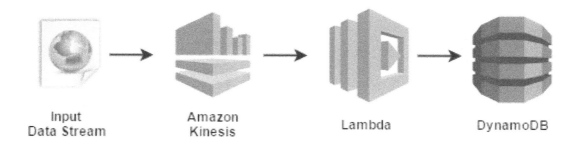

Figure 5.2: An image showing the data flow of the architecture

Suppose you run an e-commerce company and want to contact customers that put items in to their shopping carts but don't buy them. You can build a Kinesis stream and redirect your application to send information related to failed orders to that Kinesis stream, which can then be processed using Lambda and stored in a DynamoDB database. Now, your customer care team can look into the data to get the information related to failed orders in real time, and then contact the customers.

Here are the steps to perform this exercise:

1. Go to **AWS services** and search for **Kinesis**. Once it has been selected, you will be redirected to the **Kinesis dashboard**. Here, you can view the services that have been created for all four different flavors of Amazon Kinesis:

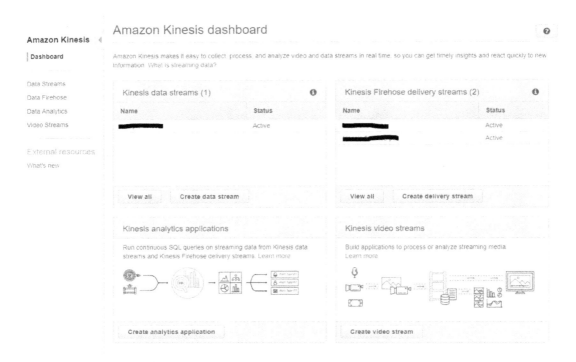

**Figure 5.3: A screenshot of the Amazon Kinesis dashboard**

> **Note**
>
> Our focus for this exercise is Kinesis Data Streams. We will look at other Kinesis services later in this chapter.

2. Go to **Data Streams** and click on **Create Kinesis stream**:

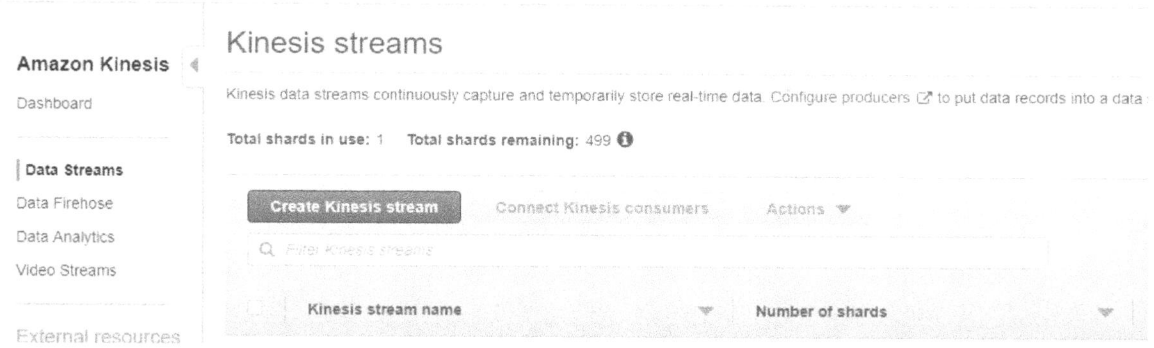

**Figure 5.4: A screenshot showing how to create Kinesis streams**

3. Provide the name of the Kinesis stream. Let's name it **kinesis-to-dynamodb**. Also, provide the estimated number of shards that you will need to handle the data. As we discussed earlier, read and write capacities are calculated based on the number of configured shards. Since we are creating it for demonstration purposes, let's put its value as 1.

You will notice that the values against write and read get changed based on the number being provided against the number of shards. Once you are done, click on **Create Kinesis Stream**:

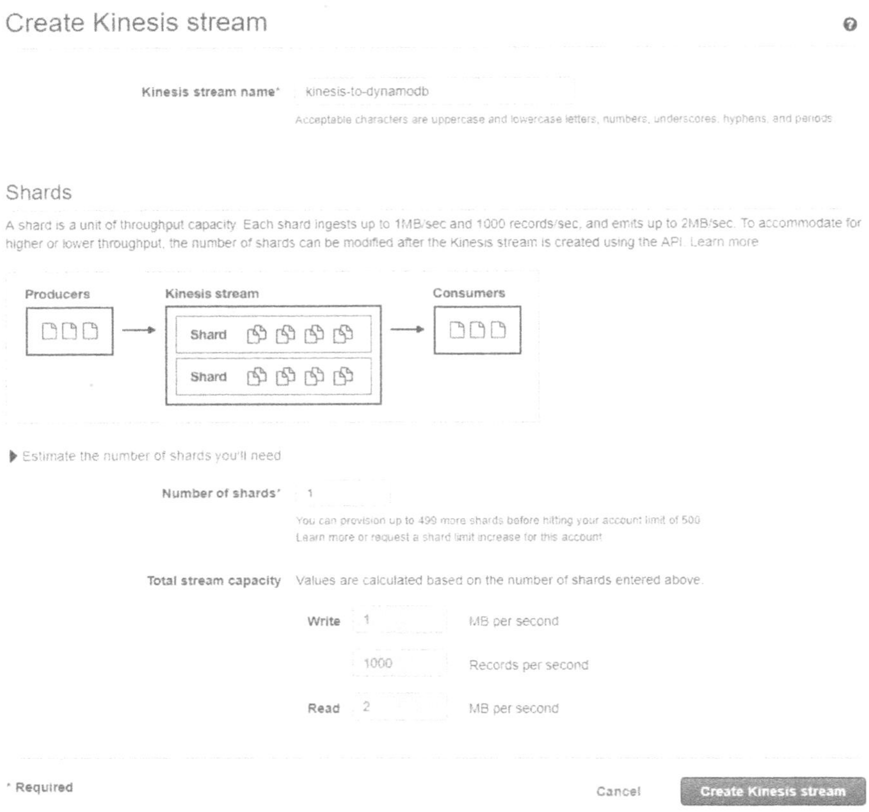

Figure 5.5: A screenshot showing the process of naming the Kinesis stream and estimating the number of shards

4. Once the stream has been created, you will notice the status of the stream as **Active**. Now, you are ready to use this stream for your incoming data:

Figure 5.6: A screenshot showing the status of the stream after creation

So, we have created a Kinesis data stream and we will integrate it now with **DynamoDB** using an AWS Lambda function.

5. Let's go ahead and create a new table in **DynamoDB** that will store the data coming from the Kinesis Data Stream. Go to **AWS services** and search for **DynamoDB**. Then, click on **Create table**:

Figure 5.7: A screenshot showing how to create a new table

6. Name your table **sample-table** and specify the **createdate** column partition key. Click on **Create**. This will create the required destination table for you:

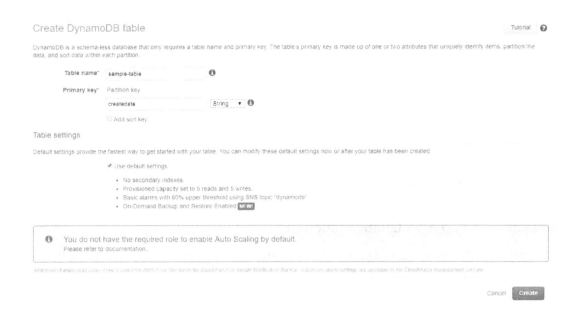

Figure 5.8: A screenshot showing the creation of the destination table

7. In the **AWS Lambda service**, write a Lambda function to fetch the records from the Kinesis data stream and store them in **DynamoDB**.

8. Click on **Create function** under **Lambda service**. Click on **Blueprints** and search for **kinesis-process-record**. Click on **kinesis-process-record template**:

Figure 5.9: A screenshot showing the creation of the function under the Lambda service

9. Give a name to the Lambda function. Create a new role, which will allow Lambda to insert records into the **DynamoDB** database. Take a look at the following screenshot to find out which policies you need to attach to the role:

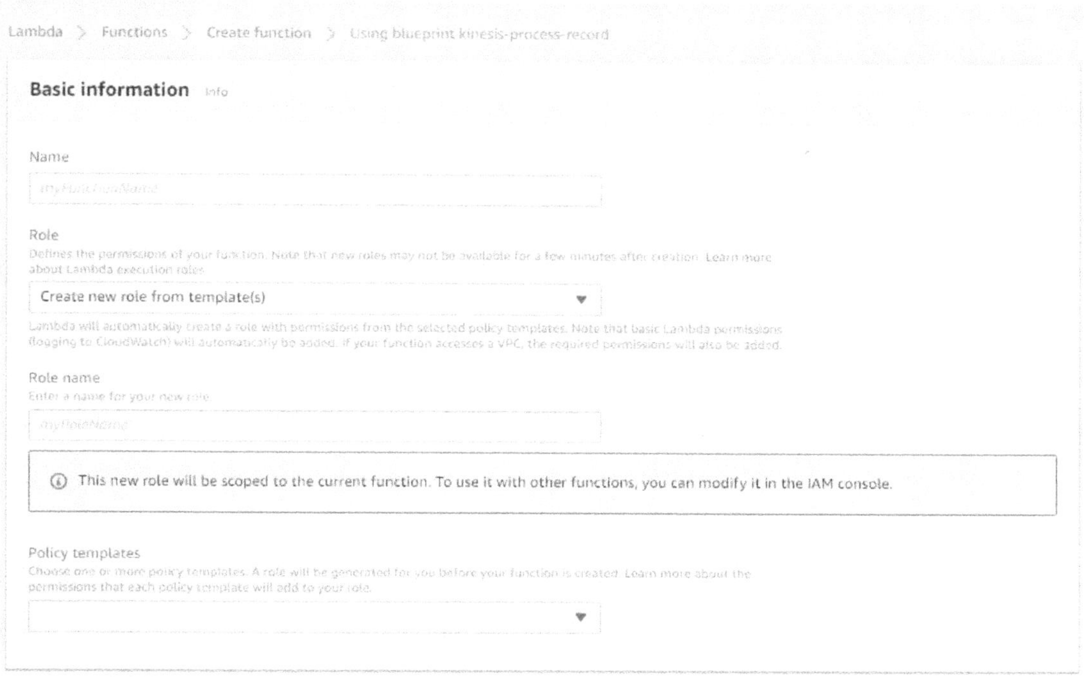

Figure 5.10: A screenshot showing the creation of a new role for the function

10. Provide the required details about the **kinesis stream**. You can set up the appropriate value of the **batch size**, depending on the flow of messages. For now, we will keep the default value. Once you are done, click on **create function**:

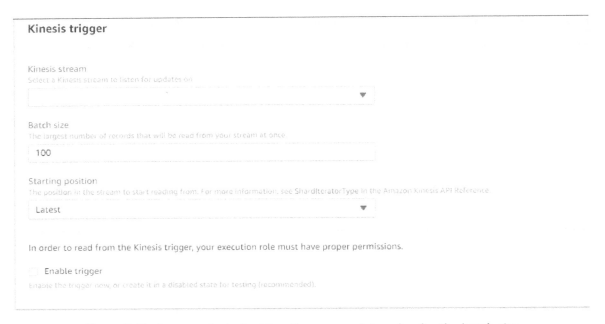

Figure 5.11: A screenshot of setting the appropriate value for the batch size

11. When you create a Lambda function from a blueprint, you need to create the function first, before changing any code.

12. Go to the section function code and replace the **nodeJS** code with the one provided in the **kinesis-lambda-dynamodb-integration.js** file.

We are populating two columns in this code. The first one is the **createdate** column, which was also defined as **PK** in our DynamoDB table definition earlier, in step 7. We are using the default value for this column. The second column is the ASCII conversion for the base64 data, which is coming in as a part of the Kinesis data stream. We are storing both values as data in our DynamoDB table, **sample-table**. Then, we are using the **putItem** method of the **AWS.DynamoDBclient** class to store the data in a DynamoDB table:

```
Goto   Tools   Window

    index.js

3
4
5   exports.handler = (event, context, callback) => {
6
7       event.Records.forEach((record) => {
8           var params = {
9               Item: {
10                  createdate: Date.now().toString(),
11                  rawdata: record.kinesis.data,
12                  message: new Buffer(record.kinesis.data, 'base64').toString('ascii')
13              },
14              },
15              TableName: 'sample-table'
16          };
17
18          doc.put(params, function(err, data) {
19              if (err) {
20                  callback(err, null);
21              } else {
22                  callback(null, data);
23              }
24          });
25      });
26  }
```

Figure 5.12: A screenshot of the code that's used to populate the two columns

13. Go ahead and save the code. To execute it, we need to create a Kinesis test event that will trigger the Lambda function and store the event data in the DynamoDB database. Click on **Configure test event**, provide a name (for example, **KinesisTestEvent**), and click on **Create**.

14. Once the test event is created, go ahead and execute the lambda function. Your lambda function should get executed successfully. Execute it couple of times and you should start seeing data into your table in DynamoDB database.

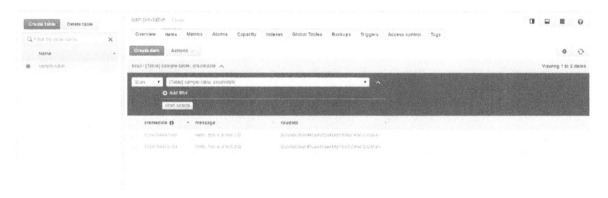

Figure 5.13: A screenshot showing the execution of the Lambda function that we created earlier

This concludes our exercise on Amazon Kinesis data events and their integration with the DynamoDB database, via the AWS Lambda service.

## Amazon Kinesis Firehose

Let's suppose you're working with stock market data and you want to run minute-by-minute analytics on the market stocks (instead of waiting until the end of the day). You will have to create dynamic dashboards such as top performing stocks, and update your investment models as soon as new data arrives.

Traditionally, you could achieve this by building the backend infrastructure, setting up the data collection, and then processing the data. But it can be really hard to provision and manage a fleet of servers to buffer and batch the data arriving from thousands of sources simultaneously. Imagine that one of those servers goes down or something goes wrong in the data stream; you could actually end up losing data.

**Amazon Kinesis Firehose** makes it easy for you to capture and deliver real-time streaming data reliably to Amazon S3, Amazon Redshift, or **Amazon Elasticsearch Service**. Using Amazon Firehose, you can respond to data in near real time, enabling you to deliver powerful interactive experiences and new item recommendations, and do real-time alert management for critical applications.

Amazon Firehose scales automatically as volume and throughput varies and it takes care of stream management, including batching, compressing, encrypting, and loading the data into different target data stores supported by Amazon Firehose. As with other AWS services, there is no minimum fee or setup cost required, so you only pay for the data being sent by you by adjusting streaming data quickly and automating administration tasks.

Amazon Firehose allows you to focus on your application and deliver great real-time user experiences rather than being stuck with the provisioning and management of a backend setup:

**Figure 5.14: A diagram showing the functionalities of Amazon Kinesis Data Firehose**

## Exercise 13: Creating a Sample Kinesis Data Firehose Delivery Stream

In this exercise, we'll go to the AWS console and create a sample Kinesis Data Firehose delivery stream. As part of this exercise, we will deliver data to an S3 bucket:

1. On **Amazon Kinesis Dashboard**, go to **Data Firehose** and click on **Create delivery stream**:

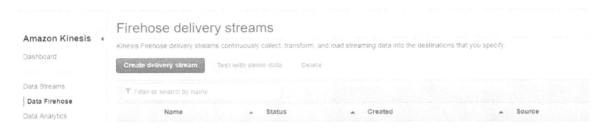

**Figure 5.15: A screenshot showing how to create a Firehose delivery stream**

2. Provide the delivery stream's name. Let's call it `Kinesis-firehose_to_S3`. Now, there are two options here to specify the source of data. The first one is **Direct PUT**, which you can use as a source if you want to send data directly from applications, such as IOT, CloudWatch logs, or any other AWS application. The second one is the **Kinesis Stream**, which you can use if you have data coming via a regular Kinesis stream. Let's take **Direct PUT** as the source for this exercise. We will discuss using a Kinesis stream as a data source in a later part of this chapter:

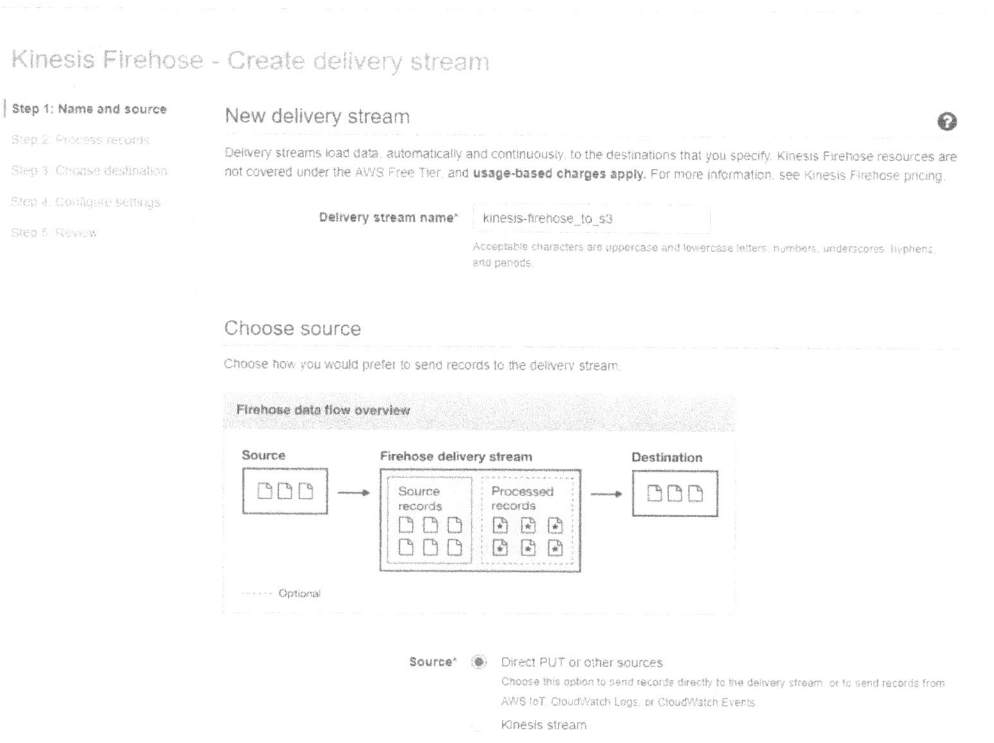
Kinesis Firehose - Create delivery stream
Step 1: Name and source
Step 2: Process records
Step 3: Choose destination
Step 4: Configure settings
Step 5: Review
New delivery stream
Delivery streams load data, automatically and continuously, to the destinations that you specify. Kinesis Firehose resources are not covered under the AWS Free Tier, and usage-based charges apply. For more information, see Kinesis Firehose pricing.
Delivery stream name*
kinesis-firehose_to_s3
Acceptable characters are uppercase and lowercase letters, numbers, underscores, hyphens, and periods.
Choose source
Choose how you would prefer to send records to the delivery stream.
Firehose data flow overview
Source
Firehose delivery stream
Destination
Source records
Processed records
Optional
Source*
Direct PUT or other sources
Choose this option to send records directly to the delivery stream, or to send records from AWS IoT, CloudWatch Logs, or CloudWatch Events.
Kinesis stream

Figure 5.16: A screenshot showing how to specify the source of data

Click **Next** to go to **Step 2: Process records**.

3. On this page, you can transform the records as required. As we discussed earlier in this chapter, Firehose allows you to do **ETL** with streaming data. To do the transformations, write a Lambda function. Let's skip this option for now:

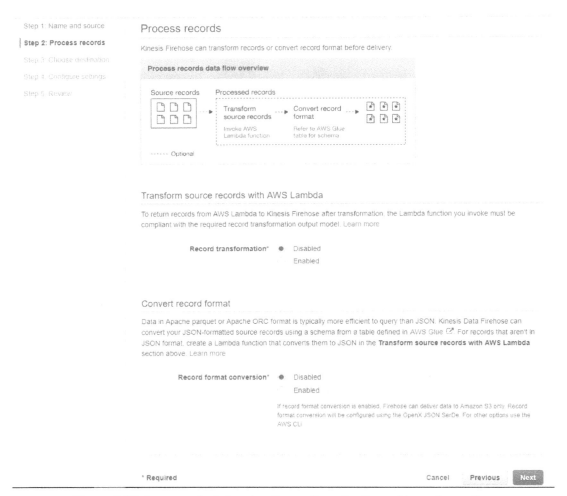

Figure 5.17: A screenshot showing the options for Record transformation

Just click on **Next** to move to **Step 3: Choose destination**.

4. Kinesis Firehose also allows you to convert data formats on the go (for example, Parquet to JSON). You can write a Lambda function to easily achieve this. Let's skip this option for now, and click on **Next** to move to **Step 4: Configure settings**.

5. On this page, you need to select the destination of your streaming data. As we discussed earlier, you can send your data to different destinations, such as S3, Redshift, or the Elasticsearch service. For this demo, we will choose **Amazon S3** as the destination.

Specify the S3 bucket details, such as where you want to save the data. Here, you can specify an existing bucket or create a new one. Leave the prefix blank. Once you are done, click on **Next** to move to **Step 4: Configure settings**:

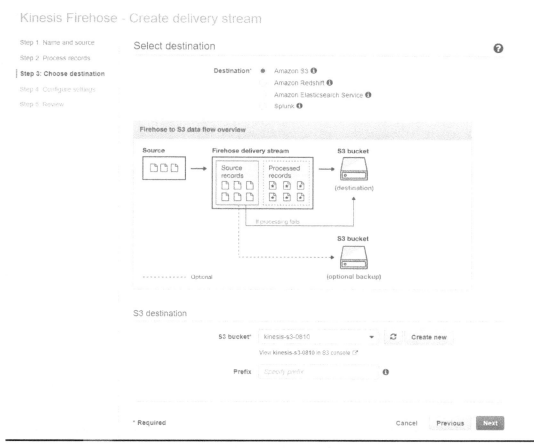

Figure 5.18: A screenshot showing how to create a new bucket or provide details about an existing one

6. Here, you can configure the **buffer conditions**, **encryption**, and **compression** settings. Buffer settings enable Firehose to buffer the records before they get delivered to S3. Let's set the buffer size as 1 MB and the buffer interval as 60 seconds. When either of these two conditions are met, the records will be moved to the destination.

Note that you can specify the buffer interval to be between 60 and 900 seconds:

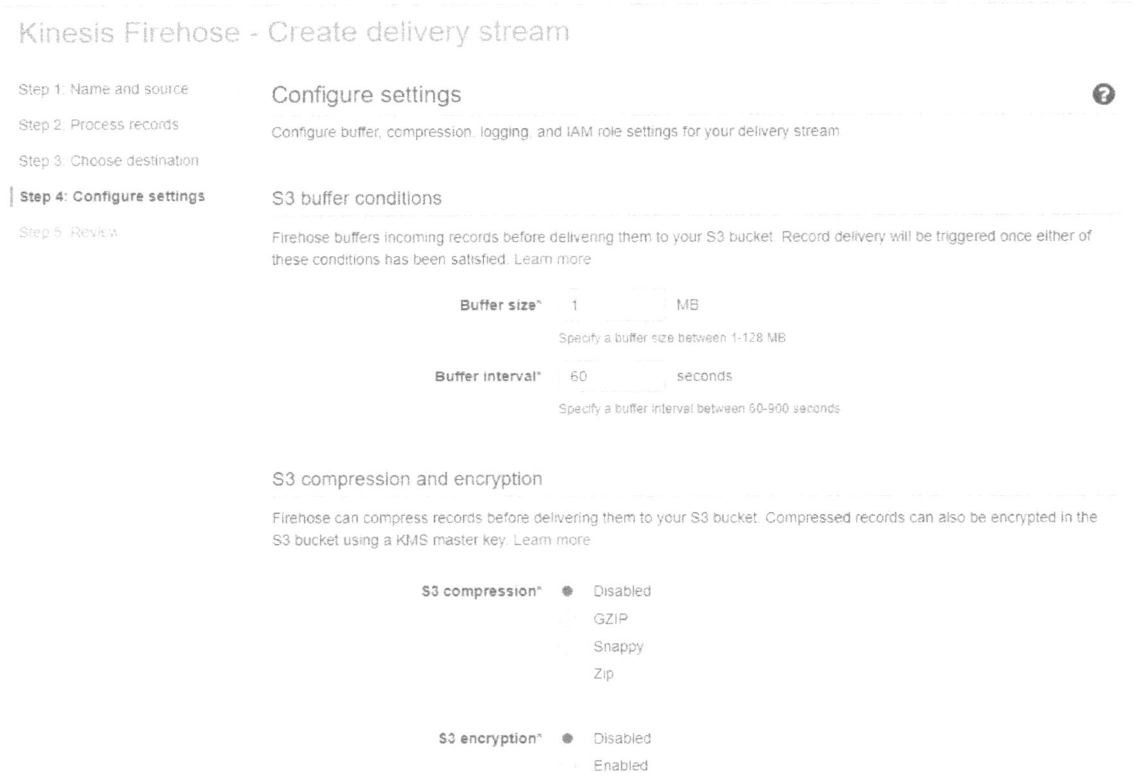

**Figure 5.19: A screenshot showing the configuration of the buffer conditions, encryption, and compression settings**

Let's keep **encryption**, **compression**, and **error logging** disabled, for now.

7. Also, you need to specify the **role** that will be used to deliver the data to S3. We will go ahead and create a new role now:

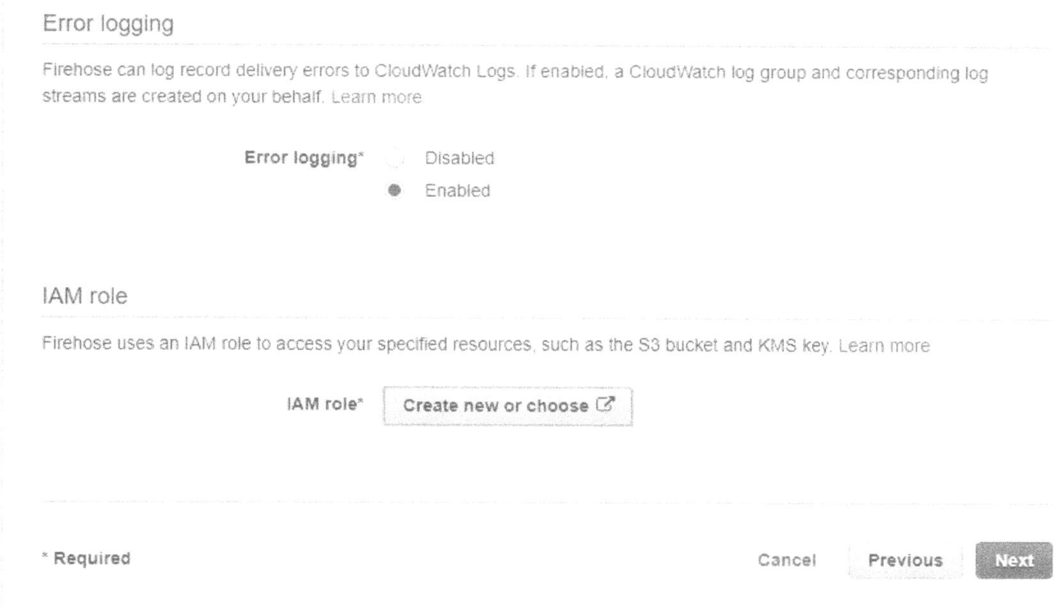

### Error logging

Firehose can log record delivery errors to CloudWatch Logs. If enabled, a CloudWatch log group and corresponding log streams are created on your behalf. Learn more

Error logging*    ○  Disabled
                  ●  Enabled

### IAM role

Firehose uses an IAM role to access your specified resources, such as the S3 bucket and KMS key. Learn more

IAM role*    Create new or choose ☑

* Required                              Cancel    Previous    Next

Figure 5.20: A screenshot showing how to specify the role that will be used to deliver the data to S3

8. At this point, we need to create a new role, so we will open a separate AWS window and search for **Roles**. Click on **Create role**. We will go back to proceed from step 6 once the role has been created (step 12):

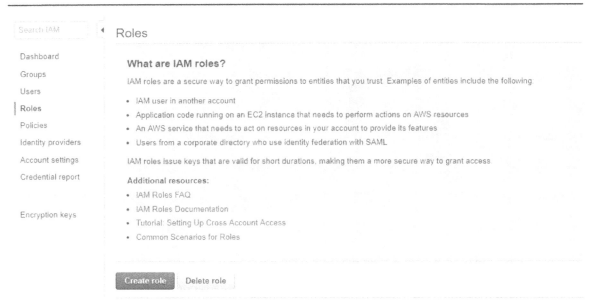

**Figure 5.21: A screenshot showing the creation of a new role**

9. Select **AWS service** under **trusted entity** and choose **Kinesis** from the list of services that will use this role. Once you select **Kinesis**, **Kinesis Firehose** will appear as the possible use case. Click on **Permissions**:

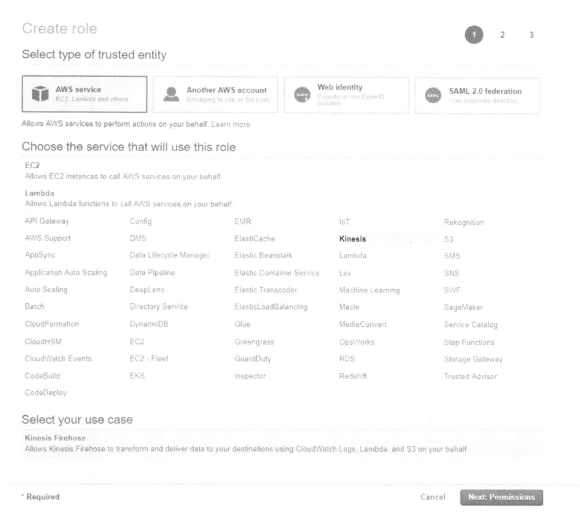

Figure 5.22: A screenshot showing the selection of the trusted entity type and service for the role

10. Attach the **Permission policy** now. Search for **S3** and attach the **AmazonS3FullAccess** policy with the role, and click on **Review**:

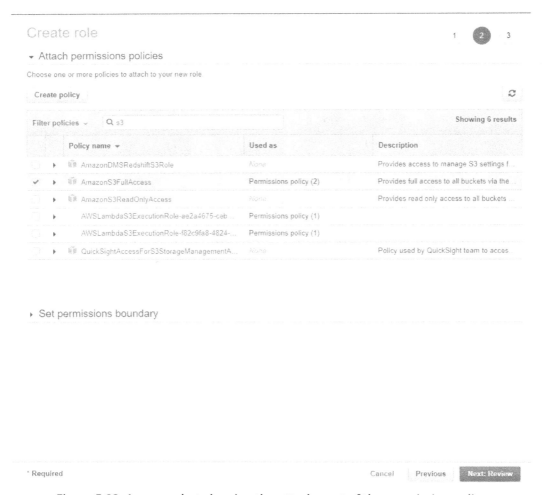

Figure 5.23: A screenshot showing the attachment of the permission policy

11. Click on **Review**. Provide a name for the role, and click on **Create role**:

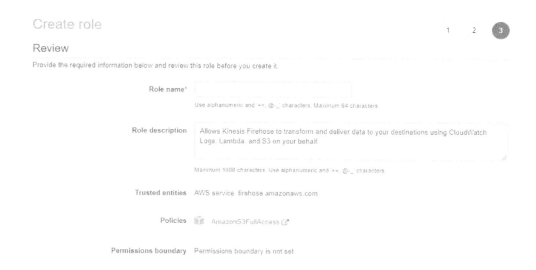

**Figure 5.24: A screenshot showing how to add the role name and description**

12. Now, the role has been created, so let's put in the required information on the screen from step 6:

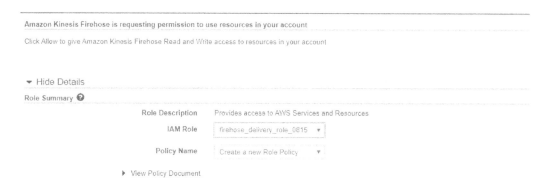

**Figure 5.25: A screenshot showing the fulfillment of details like the IAM Role and policy name**

13. Click on **Review** to verify the settings for Kinesis Firehose:

Figure 5.26: A screenshot showing the verification of settings for Kinesis Firehose

14. Click on **Create delivery stream**, and your Firehose delivery stream should be created successfully:

Figure 5.27: A screenshot showing the successful creation of the delivery stream

15. Let's try to ingest some sample data into our delivery stream and verify whether it reaches the destination.

Click on the **delivery stream** to go to the details page for that stream. Under **Test with demo data**, click on **Start sending demo data**. This will start ingesting test data into the Firehose delivery stream:

Figure 5.28: A screenshot showing the details of a particular stream

16. Once data ingestion has started, you should see the following message:

**Figure 5.29: A screenshot showing the confirmation about demo data being sent to the delivery stream**

You will have to wait for a few seconds (20 seconds) for the data to be ingested. Once data ingestion is done, you can click on **Stop sending demo data**.

17. Now, it is time to verify whether the data has been delivered successfully to S3 or not. Go to the S3 location that we configured earlier to receive the data, and you should see the data there:

**Figure 5.30: A screenshot showing the data has been successfully delivered**

Note that there might be some delay for data to appear in S3, depending on your buffer settings.

This concludes our demo of Amazon Kinesis Firehose delivery streams.

## Activity 6: Performing Data Transformations for Incoming Data

In the last exercise, we worked on a Kinesis Firehose demo that was integrated with Lambda to move real-time data into S3. You may have noticed a Lambda function in the architectural diagram, but we didn't use it in our exercise. There was a data transformation section (step 3) in the last exercise that we kept disabled.

Now, as part of this activity, we will perform data transformation for incoming data (from Firehose) by using a Lambda function, and then store that transformed data in the S3 bucket. With data transformation, we can solve many real-world business problems. We are going to create a Kinesis Firehose data stream, transform the data using a Lambda function, and then finally store it in S3. The following are some examples of this:

- Data format conversion, such as from JSON to CSV, or vice versa
- Adding identifiers
- Data Curation and Filtering
- Data enhancements, like the addition of date or time

Here are the steps to perform this activity:

1. Start by creating a Kinesis Firehose data stream, and follow the steps that we followed in the last exercise.

2. We disabled data transformation using Lambda in the last exercise. This time, enable the **Transform source records with AWS Lambda** option.

3. Once it has been enabled, create a Lambda function to do the data transformation on incoming data.

4. There are already some sample functions provided by Amazon. So, for the sake of simplicity, pick one of them, as well. Try out **General Firehose Processing**. You can read more about it on the AWS website, if required.

5. Once the Lambda function has been created, ensure that it has the required privileges.

6. Keep the rest of the settings as is.

7. Now, configure an Amazon S3 bucket as the Firehose destination, like we did in the ast exercise.

8. Send the test data from the **Test with demo data** section by clicking on **Start sending demo data**:

**Figure 5.31: The Test with demo data window**

9. Go to the S3 location that was configured earlier to receive the data, and you should see the data file. Upon downloading this data file and opening it with Notepad, you should see the data in the CSV format, as shown here:

```
TBV,HEALTHCARE,-9.54,181.46
BFH,RETAIL,0.58,17.63
IOP,TECHNOLOGY,0.43,119.19
NFLX,TECHNOLOGY,-1.23,97.77
PPL,HEALTHCARE,-0.26,30.02
WFC,FINANCIAL,-0.19,46.6
SAC,ENERGY,3.4,58.97
CVB,TECHNOLOGY,-0.65,52.17
DFG,TECHNOLOGY,1.56,137.77
WSB,FINANCIAL,-3.14,107.39
ABC,RETAIL,-0.78,24
KIN,ENERGY,-0.01,5.04
WFC,FINANCIAL,-1.36,45.24
PPL,HEALTHCARE,-1.1,28.92
WMT,RETAIL,-1.16,69.35
XTC,HEALTHCARE,-0.55,112.49
SAC,ENERGY,-2.71,56.26
JYB,HEALTHCARE,-1.77,43.45
ABC,RETAIL,0.8,24.8
IOP,TECHNOLOGY,-1.1,118.09
DFG,TECHNOLOGY,-0.36,137.41
```

**Figure 5.32: Screenshot showing data in the CSV format**

**Note**

The solution for this activity can be found on page 161.

# Amazon Kinesis Data Analytics

You are now able to consume real-time streaming data using Amazon Kinesis and Kinesis Firehose, and move it to a particular destination. How can you make this incoming data useful for your analysis? How can you make it possible to analyze the data in real time and perform actionable insights?

**Amazon Kinesis Data Analytics** is a fully managed service that allows you to interact with real-time streaming data, using SQL. This can be used to run standard queries, so that we can analyze the data and send processed information to different business intelligence tools and visualize it.

A common use case for the Kinesis Data Analytics application is time series analytics, which refers to extracting meaningful information from data, using time as a key factor. This type of information is useful in many scenarios, such as when you want to continuously check the top performing stocks every minute and send that information to your data warehouse to feed your live dashboard, or calculate the number of customers visiting your website every ten minutes and send that data to S3. These time windows of 1 minute and 10 minutes, respectively, move forward in time continuously as new data arrives, thus computing new results.

Different kinds of time intervals are used, depending on different use cases. Common types of time intervals include sliding and tumbling windows. Sharing different windows intervals is out of the scope of this book, but the students are encouraged to look online for more information.

The following diagram illustrates a sample workflow for Amazon Kinesis Analytics:

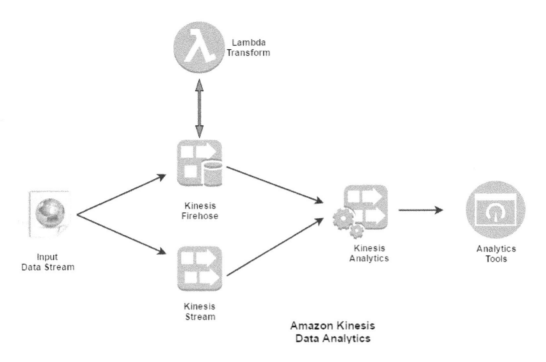

Figure 5.33: An image showing the workflow of Amazon Kinesis Analytics

You can configure the Amazon Kinesis Data Analytics application to run your queries continuously. As with other serverless AWS services, you only pay for the resources that your queries consume with Amazon Kinesis Data Analytics. There is no upfront investment or setup fee.

## Exercise 14: Setting Up an Amazon Kinesis Analytics Application

In the AWS console, set up the Amazon Kinesis Analytics application. We will also look at the interactive SQL editor, which allows you to easily develop and test real-time streaming analytics using SQL, and also provides SQL templates that you can use to easily implement this functionality by simply adding SQL from the templates.

Using a demo stream of stock exchange data that comes with Amazon Kinesis Analytics, we will count the number of trades for each stock ticker and generate a periodic report every few seconds. You will notice that the report is progressing through time, generating the time series analytics where the latest results are emitted every few seconds, based on the chosen time window for this periodic report.

The steps are as follows:

1. Go to the **Data Analytics** tab in the **Amazon Kinesis** dashboard and click on the **Create application** button to open the **Create application** form. Provide the application's name. Let's call it `kinesis-data-analytics`, and click on **Create application**. You can leave the **Description** blank:

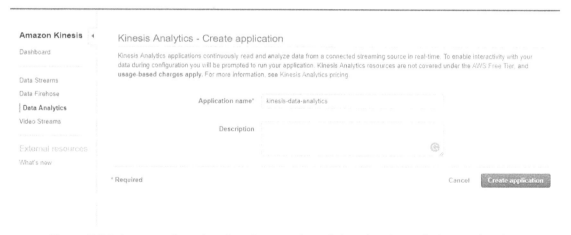

Figure 5.34: A screenshot showing the creation of the Kinesis Analytics application

2. Once the data analytics application has been created successfully, you should get the following message on the screen:

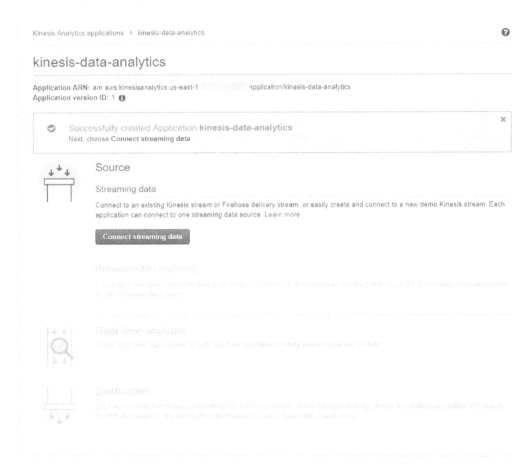

Figure 5.35: A screenshot showing the success message, stating that the Kinesis Analytics application was created successfully

3. Now, you need to connect this application with the source of the streaming data so that our analytics application starts getting data. Click on **Connect Streaming data**.

4.  You can choose either an existing **Kinesis stream** or a **Kinesis Firehose delivery stream**. Alternatively, you can configure a new stream as well. We will configure a new stream here, so let's select **Configure a new stream**:

Kinesis Analytics applications > kinesis-data-analytics > Streaming data

## Connect streaming data source

Choose from your Kinesis streams and Firehose delivery streams, or quickly configure a demo Kinesis stream that can be used to explore Kinesis Anaytics.

| Choose source | Configure a new stream |
|---|---|

Source*   ● Kinesis stream ❶
          ○ Kinesis Firehose delivery stream ❶

Kinesis stream*    Choose Kinesis stream ▼    ↻    Create new ↗

In-application stream name    In your SQL queries, refer to this source as:

SOURCE_SQL_STREAM_001

## Record pre-processing with AWS Lambda

Kinesis Analytics can invoke your Lambda function to pre-process records before they are used in this application. To pre-process records, your Lambda function must be compliant with the required record transformation output model. Learn more

Record pre-processing*    ● Disabled
                          ○ Enabled

**Figure 5.36: A screenshot showing how to connect the application with the streaming data source**

5. Click on **Create a demo stream**. This will create a new stream and populate it with sample stock ticker data:

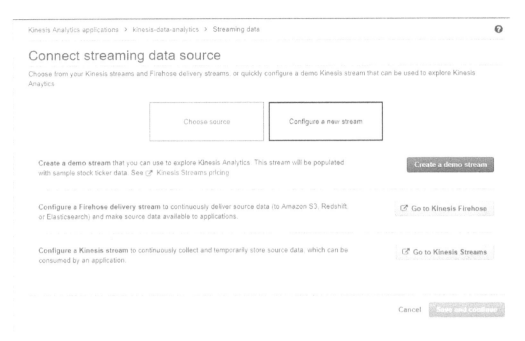

Figure 5.37: A screenshot showing the creation of the demo stream

6. As you can see in the following screenshot, new demo stream creation involves the following steps:

Creating an IAM role, creating and setting up a new Kinesis stream, populating the new stream with data, and finally, auto-discovering the schema and date formats:

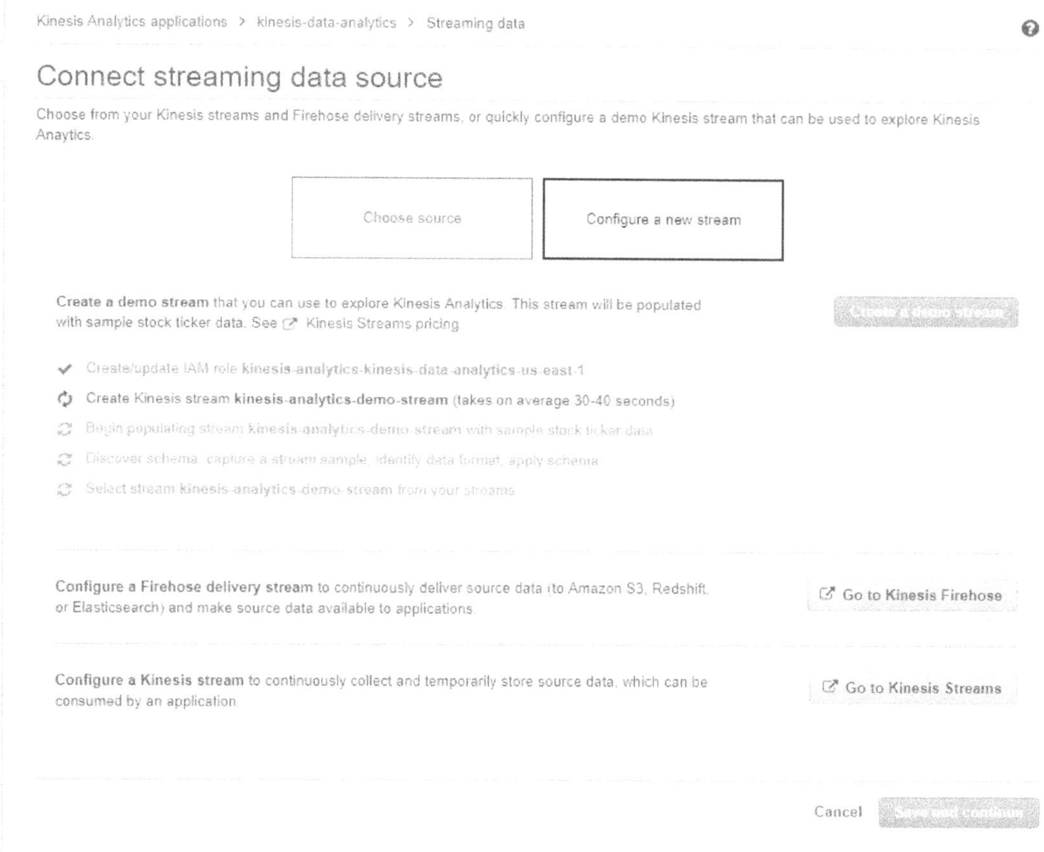

Figure 5.38: A screenshot showing the status of different processes while the demo stream is being created

7. Once the setup for the demo stream is complete, it gets selected as a source for the Kinesis data stream. The name of the stream in this example is **SOURCE_SQL_STREAM_001**. It takes you back to choosing the streaming data source, with the newly created stream selected:

**Figure 5.39: A screenshot displaying the name of the created stream, and its details**

8. Also, you will notice the sample of the data being generated by the Kinesis data stream. Please note that this schema has been auto-discovered by the Kinesis data analytics application. If you see any issues with the sample data or want to fix it, you can edit it or retry schema discovery.

We will keep the other options disabled for now and move on:

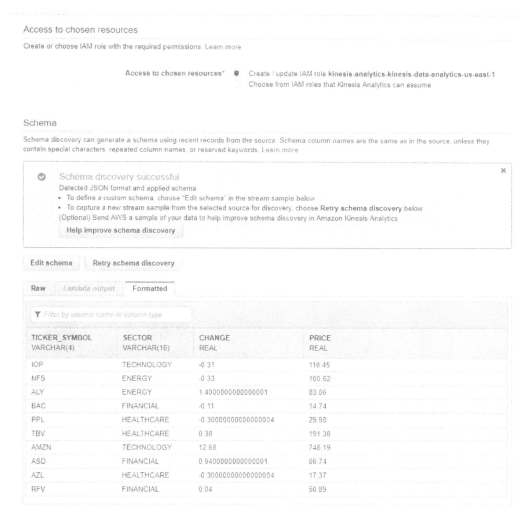

**Figure 5.40: A screenshot displaying a sample of the data generated by the stream**

9. Click on **Save and continue** and you should be redirected to the Kinesis data analytics application page. Now, the Kinesis data stream setup has been completed, and we can start configuring other settings for our data analytics application:

> **Note**
>
> You have the option to connect reference data with the real-time streaming data. Reference data can be any of your static data or output from other analytics, which can enrich data analytics. It can be either in JSON or CSV data format, and each data analytics application can be attached with only one piece of reference data. We will not attach any reference data for now.

Figure 5.41: A screenshot displaying the READY status of the Kinesis Data Analytics application

10. Now, we will go ahead and set up real-time analytics. This will enable us to write SQL queries or use an SQL from many templates that are available with it. Click on **Go to SQL editor** under **Real time analytics**.

Click on **Yes, start application** in the pop-up window:

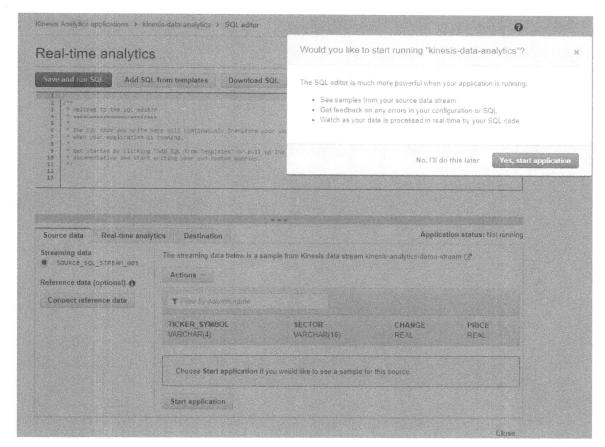

Figure 5.42: A screenshot showing the dialog box to start an application

Now, we are in the SQL editor. Here, we can see the sample data from earlier that we configured in the Kinesis Data Stream. We will also notice a SQL editor, where we can write SQL queries.

11. You can also add SQL from templates. For our demo, we will pick on SQL from the template and fetch the real-time results:

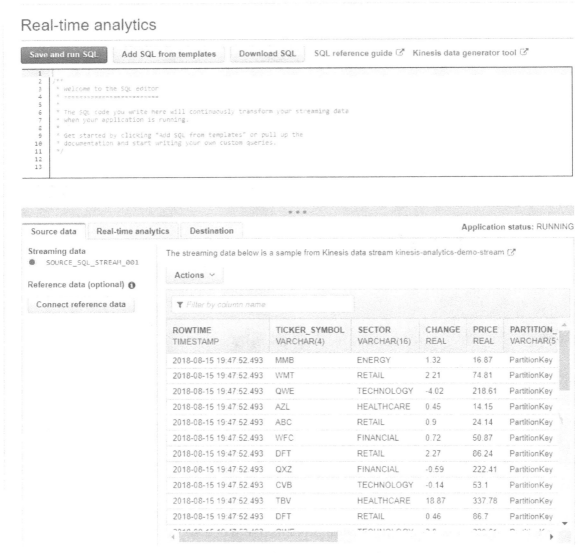

Figure 5.43: A screenshot showing the SQL editor used for writing SQL queries

12. Click on **Add SQL from templates** and choose the second query from the left, which **aggregates data in a tumbling time window**.

You will see the SQL query on the right-hand side. Click on **Add this query to the editor**:

Figure 5.44: A screenshot showing the list of SQL queries that are generated when the Aggregate function in a tumbling time window is selected

13. If you see any issue with the sample data, you can click on **Actions** to take the appropriate step:

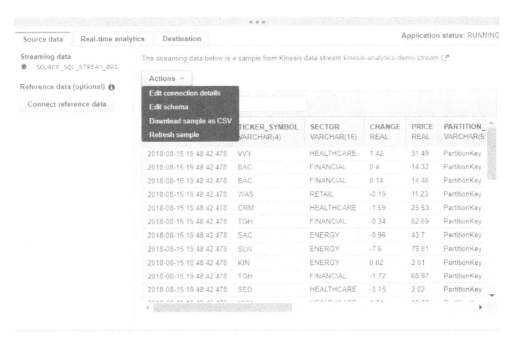

**Figure 5.45: A screenshot showing a list of different actions that can be used in case of issues with sample data**

14. Once your query appears in the SQL editor, click on **Save and run SQL**:

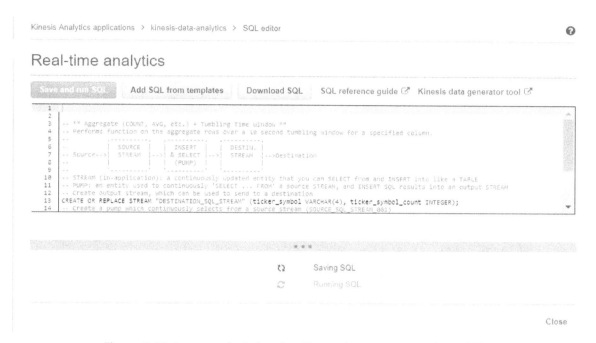

Figure 5.46: A screenshot showing the options to save and run SQL

15. Once SQL is executed against the stream data, you will start to see results, as shown in the following screenshot:

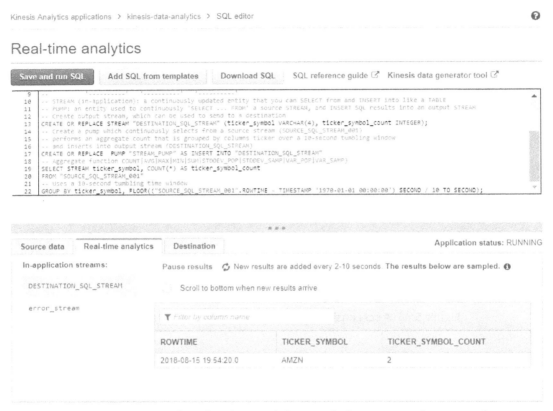

Figure 5.47: A screenshot showing real-time analytics once SQL is executed

16. Now, the Kinesis data analytics application is running this SQL against live streaming data every 10 seconds because that is the window that's specified in the SQL query. You will notice a change in the results in the following screenshot as compared to our last screenshot. This is because the results were refreshed while the screenshots were being taken:

**Figure 5.48: A screenshot showing a list of data that changes every 10 seconds**

So, you have accomplished the task of querying the streaming data in real time, using simple standard SQL statements.

17. Next, configure the destination of your real-time analysis. You can send this analysis to a Kinesis stream or a Kinesis Firehose delivery stream, and publish it on your BI dashboards. Alternatively, you can store them in Redshift or DynamoDB using the Firehose delivery stream. Go to the **Destination** tab and click on **Connect to a destination**:

Application status: RUNNING

Source data     Real-time analytics     Destination

(Optional) Connect an in-application stream to a Kinesis stream, or to a Firehose delivery stream, to continuously deliver SQL results to AWS destinations. The limit is three destinations for each application.

Connect to a destination

Close

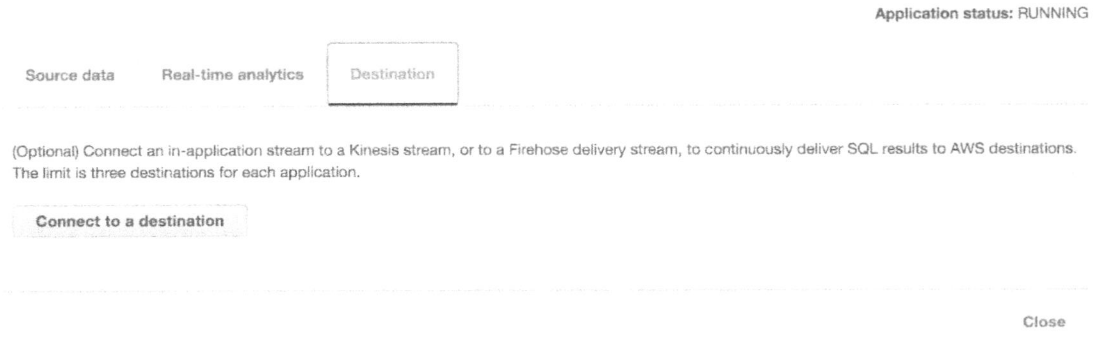

Figure 5.49: A screenshot showing the Destination tab, where an application can be connected to any stream

After clicking on **Destination**, you should see the following screenshot:

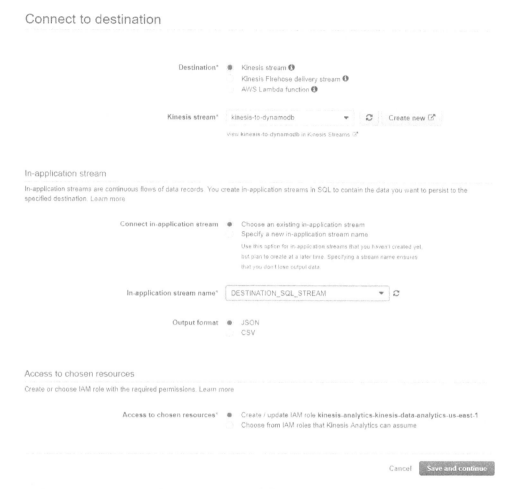

Figure 5.50: A screenshot showing the different suggested destinations once the Destination tab has been selected

18. Choose an existing Kinesis stream, and choose **DESTINATION_SQL_STREAM** for the in-application stream name; click on **Save and continue**.

Now, you have completed the setup for the Kinesis data analytics application.

19. You can review the settings for **Source**, **Real-time analytics**, and **Destination** on the application dashboard, as shown in the following screenshot. Note that at this point, your data analytics application is running real-time analytics using SQL statements on real-time data ingestion, which is happening via a Kinesis stream, and sending the query output to another Kinesis stream:

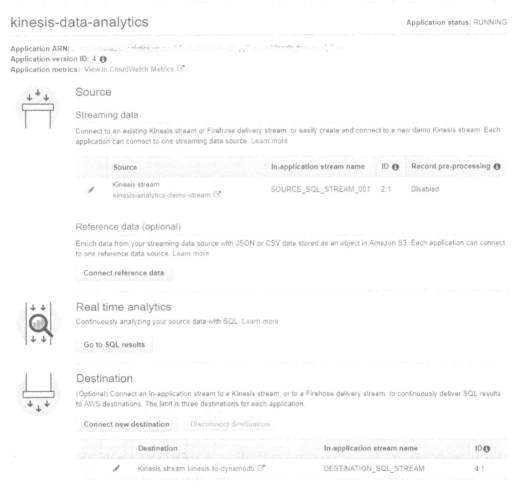

Figure 5.51: A screenshot showing the settings for the source, real-time analytics, and destination for the application

20. Once you have collected the required information, you can click on **Actions** to stop the data analytics application (and later, to start it again, as required):

Figure 5.52: A screenshot showing the status of the application once we have stopped running it

This concludes our exercise on the Kinesis Data Analytics application.

In our last exercise, we created a Kinesis Data Analytics stream, where we could analyze data in real time. This is very useful when you want to understand the impact of certain data changes in real time, and make decisions for further changes. It has many real-word applications as well, such as in dynamic pricing on e-commerce websites, where you want to adjust the pricing based on the product demand in real time.

Sometimes, there can be a requirement to join this real-time analysis with some reference data to create patterns within the data. Alternatively, you may just want to further enhance your real-time data with some static information to make better sense of your data.

## Activity 7: Adding Reference Data to the Application and Creating an Output, and Joining Real-Time Data with the Reference Data

Earlier in this chapter, we saw that the Kinesis Data Analytics application provides capabilities to add reference data into existing real-time data. In the next activity, we will enhance our test stock ticker data (that was produced natively by Kinesis Data Streams) by joining it with static data. Currently, our data contains abbreviations for company names, and we will join it with our static dataset to publish full company names in the query output.

> **Note**
>
> There is a reference data file named **ka-reference-data.json**, which is provided in the code section. This is a JSON-formatted sample file. You can use either CSV or JSON as the format of the reference data.

Here are the steps to complete this activity:

1. Make sure that you have Kinesis data analytics in working condition, and that you are able to do real-time analysis, like we accomplished in the last exercise.

2. Create an S3 bucket and upload the **ka-reference-data.json** file into the bucket.

3. Go to the Kinesis data analytics application and add the reference data. Provide the bucket, S3 object, and table details, and populate the schema using schema discovery.

4. Make sure that the IAM role is configured properly.

5. Now, you should have the real-time streaming data and reference data available in the Kinesis Data Analytics application.

6. Go to the SQL prompt and write the SQL statement to join the real-time streaming data with the reference data and out the company details whose names are provided in the reference file.

7. You should be able to see the output with both the ticker symbol and the company name as an output in real time, and it should get refreshed every few minutes.

> **Note**
>
> The solution for this activity can be found on page 165.

## Summary

In this chapter, we focused on the concept of real-time data streams. We learned about the key concepts and use cases for Amazon Kinesis Data Streams, Amazon Kinesis Data Firehose, and Amazon Kinesis Data Analytics. We also looked at examples of how these real-time data streams integrate with each other and help us build real-world use cases.

In this book, we embarked on an example-driven journey of building serverless applications on AWS, applications that do not require the developers to provision, scale, or manage any underlying servers. We started with an overview of traditional application deployments and challenges associated with it and how those challenges resulted in the evolution of serverless applications. With serverless introduced, we looked at the AWS Cloud computing platform, and focused on Lambda, the main building block of serverless models on AWS.

Later, we looked at other capabilities of the AWS serverless platform, such as S3 storage, API Gateway, SNS notifications, SQS queues, AWS Glue, AWS Athena, and Kinesis applications. Using an event-driven approach, we studied the main benefits of having a serverless architecture, and how it can be leveraged to build enterprise-level solutions. Hopefully, you have enjoyed this book and are ready to create and run your serverless applications, which will take advantage of the high availability, security, performance, and scalability of AWS. So, focus on your product instead of worrying about managing and operating the servers to run it.

# Appendix

**About**

This section is included to assist the students to perform the activities in the book.
It includes detailed steps that are to be performed by the students to achieve the objectives of
the activities.

## Chapter 1: AWS, Lambda, and Serverless Applications

### Solution for Activity 1: Creating a New Lambda Function That Finds the Square Root of the Average of Two Input Numbers

1. Click on **Create a function** to create your first Lambda function on the AWS Lambda page.

2. On the **Create function** page, select **Author from scratch**.

3. In the **Author from scratch** window, fill in the following details:

   **Name**: Enter `myFirstLambdaFunction`.

   **Runtime**: Choose **Node.js 6.10**. The Runtime window dropdown shows the list of languages that are supported by AWS Lambda and you can author your Lambda function code in any of the listed options. For this activity, we will author our code in Node.js.

   **Role**: Choose **Create new role from template(s)**. In this section, you specify an IAM role.

   **Role name**: Enter `lambda_basic_execution`.

   **Policy templates**: Select **Simple Microservice permissions**.

4. Now click on **Create function**.

5. Go to the **Function code** section.

6. Use the Edit code inline option, and enter this code:

```
exports.handler = (event, context, callback) => {
    // TODO
    let first_num = 10;
    let second_num = 40;

    let avgNumber = (first_num+second_num)/2
    let sqrtNum = Math.sqrt(avgNumber)
    callback(null, sqrtNum);
};
```

7. Click on the dropdown next to **Select a test event** in the top-right corner of the screen and select Configure test event.

8. When the popup appears, click on **Create new test event** and give it a name. Click on **Create** and the test event gets created.

9. Click on the **Test** button next to test events and you should see the following window upon successful execution of the event:

Execution result: succeeded (logs)                                                          ×
  ▶ Details

Figure 1.18: Test successful window

## Solution for Activity 2: Calculating the Total Lambda Cost

1. Note the monthly compute price and compute time provided by the Free Tier.

   The monthly compute price is $0.00001667 per GB-s and the Free Tier provides 400,000 GB-s.

2. Calculate the total compute time in seconds.

   Total compute (seconds) = 20M * (1s) = 20,000,000 seconds

3. Calculate the total compute time in GB-s.

   Total compute (GB-s) = 20,000,000 * 512MB/1024 = 10,000,000 GB-s

4. Calculate the monthly billable compute in GB- s. Here's the formula:

   Monthly billable compute (GB- s) = Total compute – Free tier compute

   $$= 10,00,000 \text{ GB-s} - 400,000 \text{ Free Tier GB-s}$$

   $$= 9,600,000 \text{ GB-s}$$

5. Calculate the monthly compute charges in dollars. Here's the formula:

   Monthly compute charges = Monthly billable compute (GB-s) * Monthly compute price

   $$= 9,600,000 * \$0.00001667$$

   $$= \$160.02$$

6. Calculate the monthly billable requests. Here's the formula:

   Monthly billable requests = Total requests – Free tier requests

   $$= 20M \text{ requests} - 1M \text{ Free Tier requests}$$

   $$= 19M \text{ Monthly billable requests}$$

7.  Calculate the monthly request charges. Here's the formula:

    Monthly request charges = Monthly billable requests * Monthly request price

    $$= 19M * \$0.2/M$$

    $$= \$3.8$$

8.  Calculate the total cost. Here's the formula:

    Total cost = Monthly compute charge + Monthly request charges

    $$= \$160.02 + \$3.8$$

    $$= \$163.82$$

# Chapter 2: Working with the AWS Serverless Platform

## Solution for Activity 3: Setting up a Mechanism to Get an Email Alert When An Object is Uploaded into an S3 Bucket

1.  Go to the AWS S3 service and click on **Create bucket**.

2.  Provide a Bucket name and select the region where the S3 bucket will be created. Click on **Next**. Note that the bucket name can't be duplicated.

3.  If you want to change any configuration, you can do it here. Click on **Next**.

4.  Now, you can change the settings related to the security of the S3 bucket. If you want to allow public access to the S3 bucket, you can uncheck the options here. Click on **Next**.

5.  Review all of the configuration settings. If you want to change anything, you can go back. Alternatively, click on **Finish** and your bucket should be created successfully.

6.  Go to the Lambda function that we created in the earlier exercise. Add **S3** as a trigger under the Lambda configuration section:

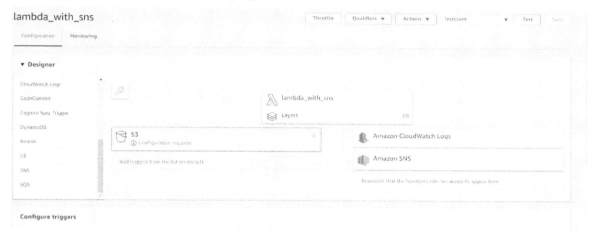

Figure 2.54: Lambda configuration window

7.  Click on **Configuration required** and add the required details related to S3 bucket configuration, mainly the bucket name. Keep the rest of the settings as default:

Figure 2.55: Configure triggers window

8. Click on Add to add that S3 bucket as a trigger to execute the Lambda function:

Figure 2.56: Window showing S3 bucket being added as a trigger

9. Click on Save to save the changes to the Lambda function:

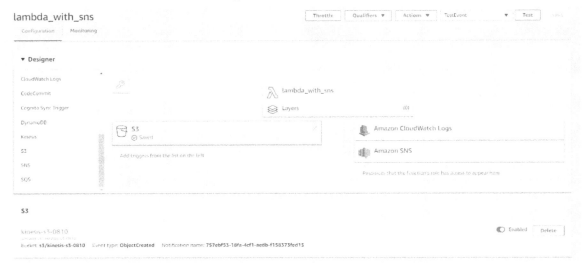

Figure 2.57: Window showing S3 bucket getting saved

10. Also, the email message will have changed in the Lambda code to reflect our activity. See line # 8 in the following screenshot. You can customize it based on your needs:

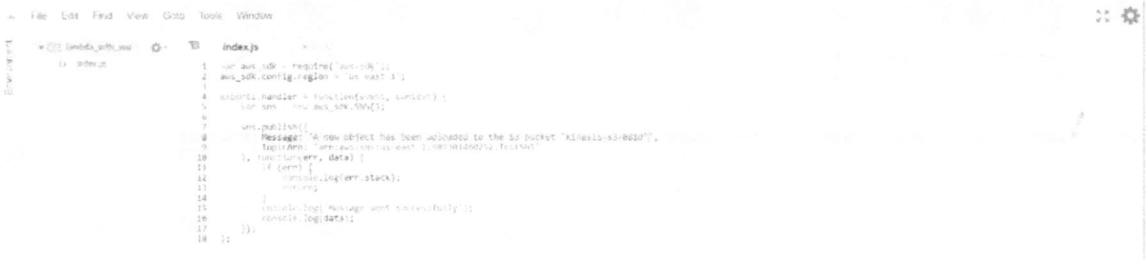

Figure 2.58: Window showing code of index.js

11. Now, upload a new sample file to the S3 bucket. You should see an email alert in your mailbox.

12. Go back to the Amazon S3 service, click on the bucket name, and click on the **Upload** button.

13. Click on **Add files** and select the file that you want to load into the S3 bucket. Click on **Next**.

14. Set the file level permissions. Click on **Next**.

15. Select the storage class. You can continue with the default option. Click on **Next**.

16. Review the configuration and click on **Upload**.

17. The file should be uploaded successfully:

**Figure 2.59: Overview section of Amazon S3**

18. Once the file has been uploaded, go to your mailbox and you should see an email alert:

**Figure 2.60: Output showing a new object being uploaded to the S3 bucket**

This concludes our activity.

# Chapter 3: Building and Deploying a Media Application

## Solution for Activity 4: Creating an API to Delete the S3 Bucket

1. Go to the AWS API Gateway console and in the API created in this chapter, create a Delete API.

2. Configure the incoming headers and path parameters properly in the Method Request and Integration Request sections.

   Your API configuration should look similar to the following screenshot:

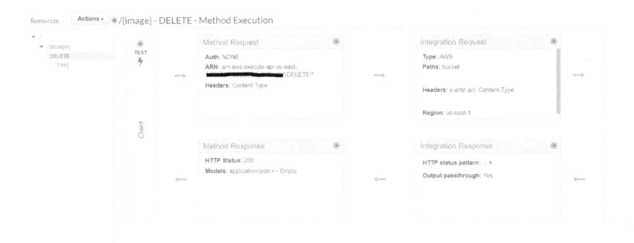

Figure 3.37: The DELETE method execution window

3. Remember to change the authorization of the **Delete** method from NONE to AWS_IAM.

4. Click on the Deploy API.

5. Test the **Delete** method using the Test Tool (Ready API). Set content-type as `application/xml`:

**Figure 3.38: Output showing the bucket getting deleted**

You should see the bucket getting deleted in the AWS S3 console.

# Chapter 4: Serverless Amazon Athena and the AWS Glue Data Catalog

## Solution for Activity 5: Building a AWS Glue catalog for a CSV-Formatted Dataset and Analyzing the Data Using AWS Athena

1. Log in to your AWS account.

2. Upload the data file **total-business-inventories-to-sales-ratio.csv** (provided with this book) into a S3 bucket. Make sure that the required permissions are in place:

**Figure 4.24: Uploading the data file**

3. Go to the AWS Glue service.

4. Select **Crawlers** and click on **Add Crawler**.

5. Provide the crawler name and click on **Next**.

6. Provide the path of the S3 bucket, where the file was uploaded in step 2. Click on **Next**.

7. Click on **Next**, as we don't want to add another data store.

8. Choose an existing IAM role that was created in *Exercise 11: Using AWS Glue to Build a Metadata Repository*. Alternatively, you can create a new one. Click on **Next**.

9. Let's keep it as `Run on demand` and click on **Next**.

10. Either you can create a new database here or click on the dropdown to select an existing one. Click on **Next**.

11. Review the settings and click on **Finish**. You have successfully created the crawler.

12. Now, go ahead and run the crawler.

13. Once the run of the crawler is completed, you will see a new table being created under the schema that you chose in step 10:

| | |
|---|---|
| **Name** | inventory_sales_ratio |
| **Description** | |
| **Database** | sampledb |
| **Classification** | csv |
| **Location** | s3://inventory-sales-ratio/ |
| **Connection** | |
| **Deprecated** | No |
| **Last updated** | Thu Nov 22 00:09:48 GMT+530 2018 |
| **Input format** | org.apache.hadoop.mapred.TextInputFormat |
| **Output format** | org.apache.hadoop.hive.ql.io.HiveIgnoreKeyTextOutputFormat |
| **Serde serialization lib** | org.apache.hadoop.hive.serde2.lazy.LazySimpleSerDe |
| **Serde parameters** | field.delim , |

Figure 4.25: The new table after the crawler run was completed

14. Go to tables, and you should see the newly created table, **inventory_sales_ratio**. Note that the table name is derived from the bucket name.

15. Go to the AWS Athena service. You should see a new table name under the database that was selected in step 10.

16. Click on new query and write the following query to get the expected output:

```
select  month(try(date_parse(observed_date, '%m/%d/%Y'))) a, count(*) from
inventory_sales_ratio
where observed_value < 1.25 group by month(try(date_parse(observed_date,
'%m/%d/%Y')))
order by a ;
```

17. When the query gets executed, you should see the expected output:

Figure 4.26: The output after the query has run

18. Looking at the output, we have a total of 8 months since 1992 where the inventories to sales ratios was < 1.25. We also have the month level count as well.

We have successfully completed the activity.

# Chapter 5: Real-Time Data Insights Using Amazon Kinesis

## Solution for Activity 6: Performing Data Transformations for Incoming Data

1. Start by creating a Kinesis Firehose Data Stream and follow the steps that we completed in the last exercise.

2. We disabled data transformation using Lambda in the last exercise. This time, enable the **Transform source records with AWS Lambda** option.

3. Once enabled, create a Lambda function to do the data transformation for incoming data:

Figure 5.54: The Transform source records with AWS Lambda window

4. There are already some sample functions that have been provided by Amazon. You can click on **Create New** and it will open up the list of transformation functions provided by AWS. Let's choose **General Firehose Processing**:

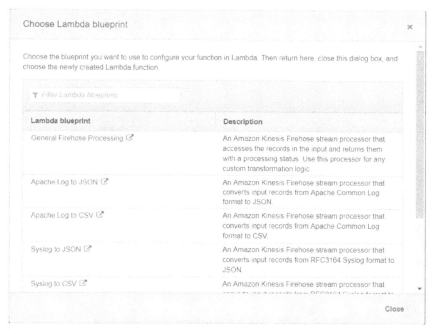

Figure 5.55: The Choose Lambda blueprint window

5. This opens up the Lambda function window. Here, you need to provide the name of the function, along with the IAM role information:

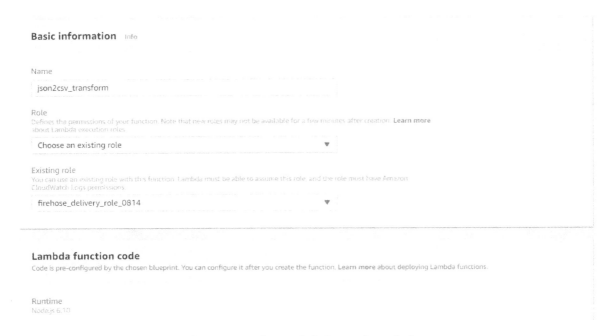

**Figure 5.56: The Basic information window**

6. Edit the code inline and replace the existing code with the code provided in the **json2csv_transform.js** file, under the code section. Keep the rest of the settings as is:

**Figure 5.57: Window showing code of index.js**

7. Once the Lambda function has been created, go back to the Firehose screen and configure the rest of the settings, such as the Amazon S3 bucket, which will work the same as the Firehose destination that we configured in the last exercise:

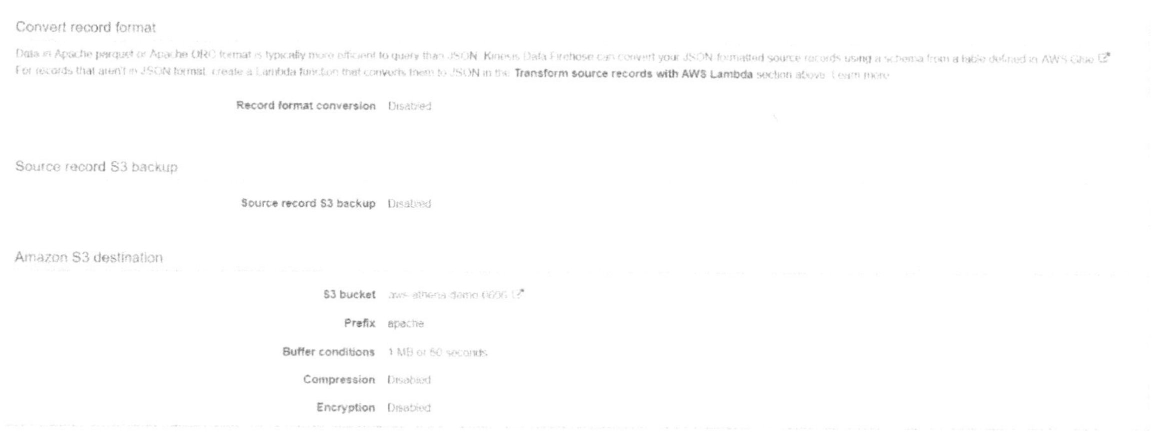

Figure 5.58: The Convert record format window

8. Also, once the Lambda function has been created, update the IAM role in the Firehose configuration to reflect the required access for the Lambda function:

Figure 5.59: The Test with demo data window

9. Everything else remains the same as in the last exercise.

10. Send the test data from the **Test with demo data** section by clicking on **Start sending demo data**:

**Figure 5.60: Window showing the Start sending demo data button**

11. Go to the S3 location that we configured earlier to receive the data and you should see the data file, as shown here:

**Figure 5.61: Window showing the data file added successfully**

12. Upon downloading this data file and opening it with Notepad, you should see the data in CSV format, as shown here:

```
TBV,HEALTHCARE,-9.54,181.46
BFH,RETAIL,0.58,17.63
IOP,TECHNOLOGY,0.43,119.19
NFLX,TECHNOLOGY,-1.23,97.77
PPL,HEALTHCARE,-0.26,30.02
WFC,FINANCIAL,-0.19,46.6
SAC,ENERGY,3.4,58.97
CVB,TECHNOLOGY,-0.65,52.17
DFG,TECHNOLOGY,1.56,137.77
WSB,FINANCIAL,-3.14,107.39
ABC,RETAIL,-0.78,24
KIN,ENERGY,-0.01,5.04
WFC,FINANCIAL,-1.36,45.24
PPL,HEALTHCARE,-1.1,28.92
WMT,RETAIL,-1.16,69.35
XTC,HEALTHCARE,-0.55,112.49
SAC,ENERGY,-2.71,56.26
JYB,HEALTHCARE,-1.77,43.45
ABC,RETAIL,0.8,24.8
IOP,TECHNOLOGY,-1.1,118.09
DFG,TECHNOLOGY,-0.36,137.41
```

**Figure 5.62: Screenshot showing data in the CSV format**

# Solution for Activity 7: Adding Reference Data to the Application and Creating an Output, Joining Real-Time Data with the Reference Data

1. Ensure that you have Kinesis Data Analytics in working condition and that you are able to do real-time analysis, like we accomplished in the last exercise:

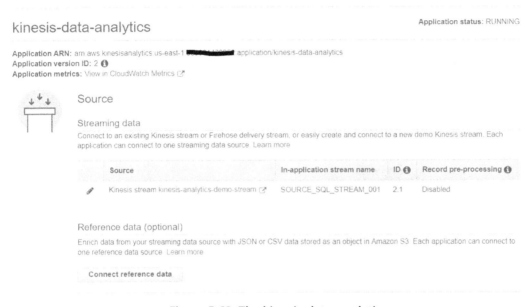

Figure 5.63: The kinesis-data-analytics page

2. Create a S3 bucket and upload the **ka-reference-data.json** file into the bucket:

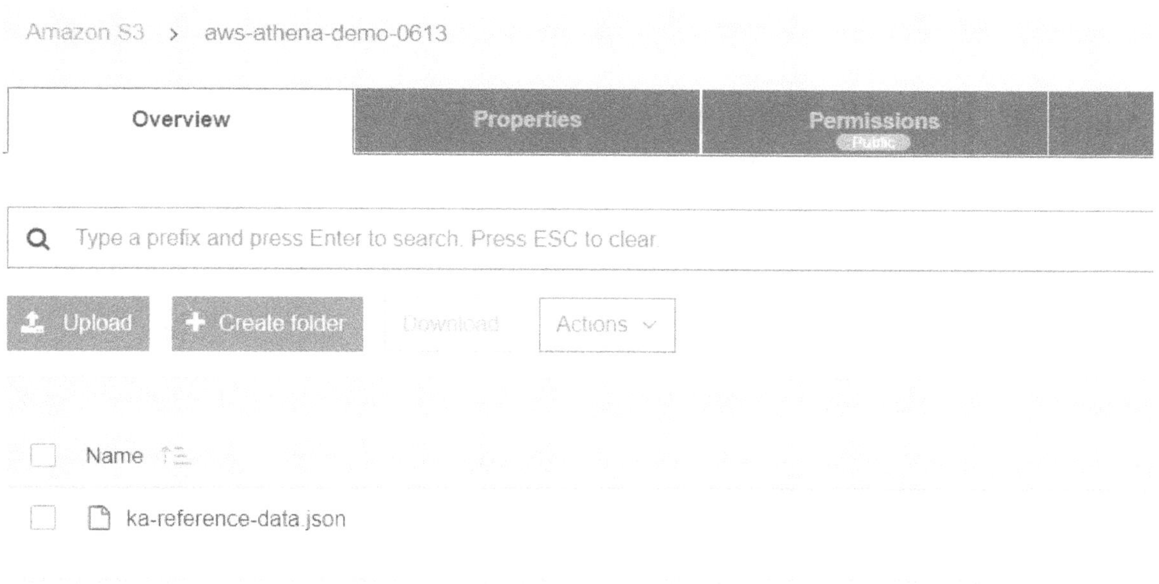

Amazon S3 > aws-athena-demo-0613

| Overview | Properties | Permissions |
|----------|-----------|-------------|

Q   Type a prefix and press Enter to search. Press ESC to clear

**Upload**   **+ Create folder**   Download   Actions ∨

☐ Name ↑↓

☐ 🗋 ka-reference-data.json

**Figure 5.64: Screenshot showing the ka-reference-data.json file added to the S3 bucket**

3. Go to the Kinesis Data Analytics application page and click on **Connect reference data**. Provide the bucket, S3 object, and table details, and populate the schema using schema discovery:

Figure 5.65: The Connect reference data source page

You will notice in the preceding screenshot that the Kinesis application will create the IAM role with required access.

Schema discovery will detect the schema for the reference data file and show you the sample data:

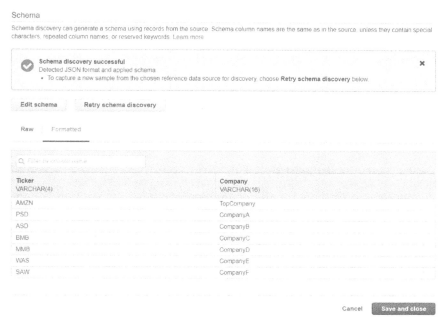

**Figure 5.66: The Schema section**

4. Click on **Save and close** button. You will have successfully added the referenced data:

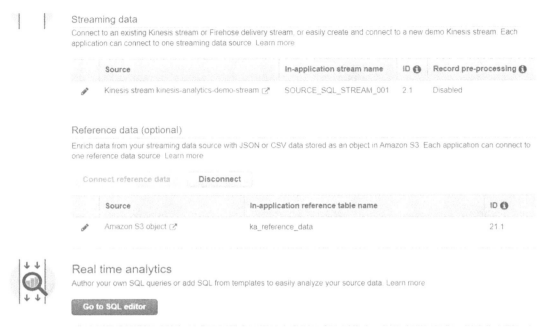

**Figure 5.67: Page showing the referenced data added successfully**

Now, you should have the real-time streaming data and reference data available in the Kinesis Data Analytics application. The following screenshot is showing real-time streaming data: The following image is showing the added reference data:

Figure 5.68: The Real-time analytics section

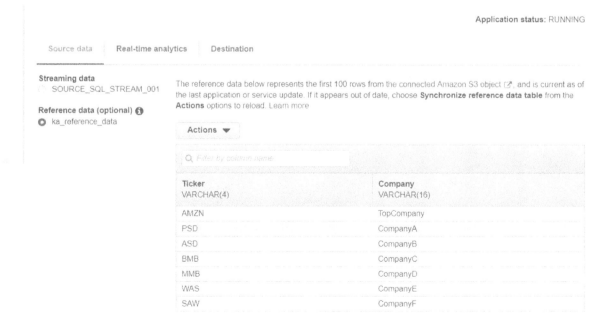

Figure 5.69: The Source data section

5. Go to the SQL prompt and write the SQL statement to join real-time streaming data with the reference data, and out the company details whose names are provided in the reference file.

6. Run the following query in the SQL prompt. In this query, we are joining (left join) **SOURCE_SQL_STREAM_001** with the **ka_reference_data** dataset and filtering where company name is not null:

```
CREATE STREAM "KINESIS_SQL_STREAM" (ticker_symbol VARCHAR(14), "Company_
Name" varchar(30), sector VARCHAR(22), change DOUBLE, price DOUBLE);

CREATE PUMP "STREAM_PUMP" AS INSERT INTO "KINESIS_SQL_STREAM"
    SELECT STREAM ticker_symbol, "kar"."Company", sector, change, price
    FROM "SOURCE_SQL_STREAM_001" LEFT JOIN "ka_reference_data" as "kar"
    ON "SOURCE_SQL_STREAM_001".ticker_symbol = "kar"."Ticker"
    where "kar"."Company" is not null ;
```

> **Note**
>
> You can use the inner join while removing the where clause to achieve the same results.

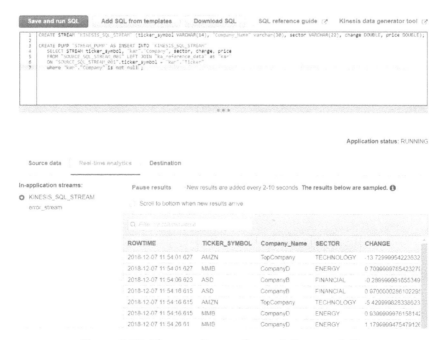

Figure 5.70: The result page for real-time analytics

7. You should be able to see the output with both the ticker symbol and company name as output in real-time. It should get refreshed every few minutes:

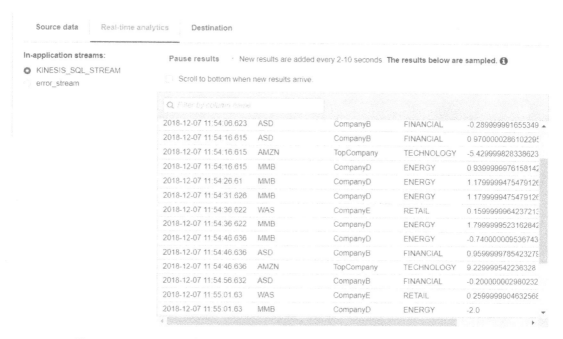

Figure 5.71: Output showing both the ticker symbol and company name

This concludes our activity on adding reference data and using it to perform real-time data analytics on Amazon Kinesis Data Analytics.

# Index

**About**

All major keywords used in this book are captured alphabetically in this section. Each one is accompanied by the page number of where they appear.

testevent: 64
testsns: 58, 64, 66
text-based: 124
textbox: 88
throughput: 6, 21,
    53-55, 124, 136
ticker: 155, 158, 173-174
timeline: 5
timely: 42
topicarn: 64, 93
tostring: 41
trades: 155
transfer: 27
transform: 8, 100, 140, 151
transforms: 100
tremendous: 70
trigger: 66-67, 94, 127, 135

# U

unchecked: 32
underlying: 5-6, 9, 16,
    27, 42, 80, 101, 104,
    112, 116-117, 121, 174
underneath: 102
understand: 2-3, 18-19, 25,
    43, 52, 55, 103, 112, 173
updates: 3, 112
upfront: 6, 27, 54, 154
upgrading: 2
us-west-: 88

# V

valuable: 124
values: 36, 54-55,
    120, 130, 134
variable: 13, 77, 80
variables: 13, 40
verify: 120, 148-150

verifying: 60
version: 24-25, 55, 112
--version: 95
versioning: 24, 30, 36
versions: 24-25, 42-43
viewing: 36
visualize: 153

# W

waiting: 136
warehouse: 100, 153
warning: 48
workflows: 7

# X

x-amz-acl: 80

# Y

yaml-based: 96

www.ingramcontent.com/pod-product-compliance
Lightning Source LLC
Chambersburg PA
CBHW080524060326
40690CB00022B/5016